NEVER
WALK
AGAIN

NEVER WALK AGAIN

My Testimony from
WHEELCHAIR to WORSHIP

GARY GOOD

Internet addresses given in this book were accurate at the
time it went to press.

This book shares the author's own recollections and
memories. He has done his best to be faithful to his
experiences, but memory is imperfect. He has also done his
best to present his journey and the other people in it in the
most honest, positive light.

Printed in the United States of America
Published in Lewistown, PA
Cover design by Christina Gaugler
Library of Congress Control Number: 2025925656

Paperback ISBN 979-8-89420-072-9
Hardcover ISBN 979-8-89420-081-1

For more information or to place bulk orders, contact the
author or the publisher at
Jennifer@BrightCommunications.net.

Bright
COMMUNICATIONS

To encourage you and let you know
when you are told you can't, God can

Contents

Preface

By Gary Good Jr.

We never meant to write a book.

This started as a simple conversation—just me and my Dad talking on a chilly morning in February of 2025. I hit "record" during our conversation—not to put him on the spot, but because his testimony needed to be heard.

Over the years, my dad had shared bits and pieces of what happened to him on October 15, 2000. A tragic car accident. A life-changing diagnosis. A long road to recovery. But even then, I still didn't know the whole story. I didn't know what it felt like to be upside down in a Jeep with the world spinning around you. I didn't know what it felt like to be stuck in a hospital bed for months, watching family, friends, and physicians walking in and out, leaving you behind again and again. I didn't know what it meant to hear the words, "You'll never walk again."

And I definitely didn't know what it would take to prove them all wrong.

I'll never forget the day we sat down. My dad and I were at his home in Bucks County, Pennsylvania. The winter weather was finally breaking, and it was starting to be a beautiful day. We sat at the dining room table. I asked him some questions. And then I listened.

This book is the result of that conversation. It is the story of my father, Gary Good Sr.—someone who faced what most people would call the end. Yet, he somehow found the strength to start over, from ground zero. He shattered his C5 and C6 vertebrae and broke every single one of his ribs. According to statistics related to his type of spinal cord injury, he had about a one in a million chance of recovery.

But he did just that.

His story is a testimony for *anyone* who's been told "you can't." It's for anyone who's been knocked down, left behind, or feels defeated. This message is for anyone who's been paralyzed by fear, pain, or circumstance. It's for anyone who's ever felt abandoned in their struggle because he knows that place very well and managed to escape its grasp.

Somewhere between broken bones and lost hope, my father discovered something greater than recovery. He found *relationship*—with himself, with the people who refused to let him go, and most importantly, with God.

We pray that reading this book restores *your* faith in your ability to walk again—whether literally or figuratively. We hope you see that some miracles develop slowly, revealing themselves quietly over months of silent progress, incremental gains, and the smallest of victories.

And I pray that you realize something I discovered along the way:

My father didn't just survive the accident.

He was born again from it.

Join me for a ride in the driver's seat of that Jeep on the night of his car accident. Feel the vibrations cast by his recollection of the events. These memories will reignite your desire to walk with a purpose. Let's rewind back to the moment when a ten-mile drive almost cost my father his life—and ultimately led to his destruction, reconstruction, and brand new relationship with God.

My family

Left to right: My older sister, Regina; my younger brother, Gerard; my mother, Jean; my younger sister, Roseann; and me, at Mediterraneo's in Bayonne, New Jersey, in November 1997

Chapter 1

The Night Everything Changed

October 15, 2000, was the kind of night you convince yourself to call it an early one. That kind of night when your instinct tells you to stay home.

But love has a way of overriding all of that. I had no plans on leaving my warm, comfortable house that night. I owned a two-family home on Wallis Avenue in Jersey City, New Jersey. I was looking forward to a good night's sleep so I would be better by the morning.

I was battling a cold and definitely needed to recharge. It was really uncommon for me to get sick. At that time in my life, I took great care of myself. I knew that a good night's sleep was the best medicine for fighting off that sickness, and I was confident that I'd be back to myself in no time.

It had been a long, difficult week at the prison where I worked as a Correction's Officer. I was dozing off because of the fatigue and needed a break from working overtime to catch some solid rest. I was excited to spend time with my eight year-old son, Gary Jr., the next day. He was with his mom that night because we shared custody of him. It was going to be my weekend, so I was getting ready to hang out with my little guy the next day. Even though things didn't work out between me and his mother, I did my best to spend every chance I got with my son because it was important to me as a father.

At that point in my life, I was laser-focused on providing a healthy and happy life for Gary Jr. My days were consumed by working doubles and working out. I was into mixed martial arts, dedicated to self-care, and I was in excellent physical shape—maybe the best of my entire life. I felt invincible. Bulletproof.

It made me proud to share my love of sports and fitness with Gary Jr. He was already enrolled in both baseball and karate. I wanted to instill in him the same morals and values that my father had shared with me.

Those same morals and values were instrumental in my upbringing and also in becoming the man I am today. My father emphasized them to me and reinforced that our elders and neighbors were not simply people passing through our lives, but an extended part of our family—concerned, supportive, and deserving of respect. Those lessons formed the foundation of my character, teaching me that compassion and consideration ripple outward while also strengthening every bond within.

My father definitely showed me a tireless work ethic, which I used for my approach with baseball. I was committed to improving and delivering, rather than just treating it like a game.

My father's philosophy was that discipline and effort would always bring results. His voice still echoes in my mind when it comes to money and ambition: "If you want things in life, you have to get up and go get them. Prioritize for the future and monitor your spending." Those words shaped my approach to work and to every other challenge I encountered. They reminded me that success is built upon consistent effort, thoughtful choices, and the support of the people around us.

That evening, at around 9 p.m., my phone buzzed with a call from my younger brother, Gerard. The temptation to let it go to voicemail was strong, but we were raised better. Our bond was built on trust and looking out for one another.

When Gerard was fourteen, living with my parents who retired in Florida, he began wrestling with the idea of dropping out of high school early. As his older brother, I made it my mission to encourage him, to remind him of his potential and push forward by his side. I urged him to finish school, work hard, and believe in a brighter future. Over the years, that understanding became our foundation and a constant reminder that *no one fights alone*.

Picking up the phone that night was more than just answering a call. It was reaffirming that unspoken promise that we would always lift each other up, no matter how tough the journey became.

"What's up, G," I said.

"Hey, man. Tony, Mike, and I want to go shoot some pool at the After Hours," Gerard said.

"We're headed up to your place now," the other two chimed in.

I sensed that they could probably use a designated driver so I didn't fight it. "Oh, yeah?" I replied, trying to shake the sleep from my brain, remembering the After Hours was on Staten Island, about a half hour away.

"Yeah, man, come out with the boys," they replied, as they continued toward my house.

"It's after nine," I said, holding my phone away from my ear to check the time. "I was practically asleep on the couch."

"C'mon, mannn," they all persisted.

The decision was made. I could tell by their voices that nobody was in the shape to drive. By this point, I'd known them for years. Tony worked as a warehouse manager, and Mike worked in the trucking industry as a shop steward. Those friends were like family.

I really didn't want to leave. My gut urged me to stay home. *Just say no.* But of course, I had to go. I knew I wouldn't be able to live with myself if I didn't drive them and they were injured—or worse. I needed to get them safely to the pool hall.

"Alright … give me a few. I'll be right down."

Before I knew it, they were knocking on my door. This shouldn't have been surprising because they only stumbled over from Mike's house down the block.

Initially, I was frustrated because I really needed to rest off my head cold, but once I saw the condition they were in, I knew for sure I had to step up and get them there safely. I unlocked the door, and the three of them spilled into my house, laughing and carrying on with their conversation from outside.

Yeah, there's no way I'm letting them get behind the wheel, I thought, validating my decision to drive them to the pool hall myself. There's nothing wrong with "feeling nice," but from my experience, it was in their best interest to have a designated driver.

As a Corrections Officer for six years for Hudson County Corrections Department in

Jimmy Orrico, Gary Jr., and me

South Kearny, New Jersey, I had seen and heard of unimaginable stories from car accidents. In my job, I formed close bonds with my coworkers, many of whom became like brothers to me. One in particular was Jimmy Orrico. We attended the police academy together, stayed in the same barracks, worked out together at the gym, and painted the town red at clubs after we came home.

Jimmy's parents, Gloria and Carmine Orrico, adopted me like one of their own. They were an amazing support system, always showing up when I needed it most. Their door was always open, filled with love, the aromas of home-cooked meals, and even some snacks to fuel our long study sessions. It was more than the food and snacks though; it was their genuine care and belief in us that fueled our fires as we powered through the police academy.

Gloria and Carmine never let us forget that success was a collective effort. Their faith in us remained a guiding light, reminding me that family often extends beyond bloodlines to include those who choose to stand by us, nourish us, and help us reach our full potential.

Considering the training I received in the academy and my life experiences, it didn't take much for me to figure out what needed to be done. Despite everything telling me to stay home, my family needed me. I wasn't about to let them down.

I shrugged on a windbreaker, grabbed my car keys, and stepped outside into the cool air of an October night in Jersey City.

I don't even wanna go, I thought to myself as I followed them out of my house, reaching behind me to make sure the door was closed and locked securely. It was already a long day, and I was *beat*. But I remembered my father's direction: Protect the family at all costs.

"Save your gas, bro! You can drive the Jeep," Tony called to me, gesturing with the keys in his right hand toward his burgundy Jeep Cherokee parked out front.

"Thanks, bro," I said. I preferred driving my own vehicle, but I didn't want to make it a big deal. There was no point in arguing when the main objective was to get them to and from the pool hall safely. *Every penny helps,* I thought.

I was working overtime, saving money for home repairs and new adventures with my son. It wasn't that far of a drive, but my car wasn't great on gas, so it wouldn't hurt to save a few bucks. I tried to focus on the positives to take my mind off the stress I was feeling.

"I'll take shotgun," Tony said, leaving Gerard to sit behind me while Mike sat in the rear passengers seat of the Cherokee. Gerard and Mike didn't complain about being in the backseat. They were too busy jammin', laughing, and having a good time.

It was hard to ignore, and their bursts of high energy dampened what little I had left. I was feeling more tired by the second, and the beginnings of a headache were starting to form behind my eyes.

"You sure you guys still wanna go?" I asked, really just hoping they'd say no.

"Oh yeah," I heard from the backseat.

I fired up the Cherokee, and the radio sprang to life. Mike was a DJ, and they were all into techno, high energy music.

This isn't going to help my headache, I thought. As I went to put the Jeep in drive, double checking that everyone was buckled up and ready to go, the guys started telling me about their day leading up to now. I listened as they continued laughing and joking around.

"Last call, should I whip it around the block and drop you guys off home?" I shot once more before leaving for Staten Island.

"Nah, come on. Let's go shoot pool for a little bit and hang out," Mike responded. I remember him talking around the cigarette that was hanging from his lip—one of his signature moves.

"Alright, let's make moves," I muttered as I tried to tune them out and focus on the drive.

Next thing I knew, we were driving down Wallis Avenue and heading toward Route 440. I took that all the way up to route 169, toward Bayonne and the Staten Island Bridge. The bridge to New York was covered in fog, but I could see it ahead in the distance. I was carefully below the speed limit, but the weather and lights outside created a surreal blurriness around the Jeep in the dark.

I turned up the radio to distract me from the joking going on in the Cherokee.

I carefully turned onto route 169, around a circle, leaving the traffic behind us. Two lanes were about to merge into one. It was late. The road was quiet. I started thinking about what I'd do once I got back home. *Throw my keys. Kick off my shoes. Fall asleep, face first. Not necessarily in that order though.*

That's when it happened.

I was holding steady around 50 mph, the radio buzzin', when I noticed the lanes start to narrow ahead. All of a sudden, the bright headlights of an 18-wheeler appeared in my rearview mirror.

The other driver was basically glued to my bumper and refused to ease off for the merge. My knuckles whitened around the steering wheel as the distance shrank between us and the outcome became obvious.

The impact was like an explosion. Our Jeep was rear-ended by the truck with so much force that we were launched forward. When I tried to swerve away from the truck, the Jeep started flipping. We hit a divider, then continued to flip. Relentlessly.

Once. Twice. Over and over, we rolled like a Hollywood action scene.

Everything was sudden. Time froze. As the metal got crushed, the glass was shattered, and bones were fractured. In a split-second, our entire world was flipped upside down.

Then—silence.

The Cherokee finally stopped tumbling just short of the bridge's edge. A few more feet, and we would've fallen to our death in the filthy water below us.

I tried to look around inside the crushed Jeep, but I was so disoriented by the accident and the flipping and the shock that it took me a few minutes to comprehend that I was hanging upside down. I was still wearing my seatbelt, which was now choking me and cutting off my air. The ringing in my ears was so loud it sounded like a siren. The air was thick with smoke and dust from the broken glass.

"Gerard! Mike! Tony!" I yelled, coughing in between.

No answer.

I tried to grab my seatbelt with my right hand to pull it away from my neck and get more air, but my arms hung like lead weights at my sides. Next attempt, I went to shake my legs to see if I could free myself that way, but they wouldn't move either.

Panic began to slow my heartbeat. *Oh my God*, I thought. I hadn't prayed in a very long time—not since going to Catholic church with my family as a child. But that was my first thought in that moment of desperation.

I saw Tony next to me. He was also hanging upside down. A quick glance in the rearview mirror revealed that so were Gerard and Mike. None of them were moving. *Are they breathing?* I couldn't tell.

I wasn't really able to move to investigate further because the front seat had broken off from the floor mounts. The seatbelt had me tied up in a knot while holding me upside down.

Reflexively, I reached for my phone to call for help. It felt like I was moving in slow motion, under water. I started to feel the sensation of pins and needles down my leg.

I must've broken my leg, I thought.

Just then, a car raced up beside the Jeep and screeched to a halt.

"Don't move!" the man yelled. "We called for an ambulance and the police!"

The wait for help to arrive felt like forever. The tingling in my leg and now both my arms was getting worse.

There still weren't any sounds coming from inside the car. No movement or any signs of life around me. Not from Tony. Not from Gerard. Not even Mike in the back. I looked back and realized that Mike still had a broken cigarette hanging from his lip.

"Wow, you kids can't even take a punch," I groaned, jokingly, hoping they'd laugh.

No response.

"Is this really happening? I couldn't tell.

It was way too quiet in the Jeep. But inside my head, I could still hear that terrible siren-like ringing. All of a sudden, it was combined *with* sirens—followed by red, white, and blue flashing lights cutting through the darkness.

First responders swarmed the wreck. They sounded like they were yelling at each other from a distance, as I tried to make out what they were saying and understand the severity of the crash. My head felt like it was covered in bubble wrap and duct taped all over. I could barely hear the first responders, let alone understand what they were saying. Even though it felt like hours to me,

I later learned they had arrived within twenty minutes.

"Are you okay?" asked the first EMT to reach the Jeep. "What's the matter?"

"I think I broke my arms and my leg," I said. "They're numb."

More EMTs came to assist with getting me out of the Jeep, but they were unable to get me free.

"Don't move!" yelled a firefighter as he raced up to the Jeep, holding out both of his hands in the STOP maneuver. "Stay where you are!"

The EMTs and firefighters turned their attention to Gerard, Mike, and Tony. They pulled them out of the Jeep quick and made it look easy. I lost track of what happened to my brother and friends at that point because all of the first responders shifted their focus back to me.

"Try not to move," the firefighter repeated, now with an edge to his voice. As I tried to calm my body—and the overwhelming panic—they started up the Jaws of Life to rip apart the Jeep, going up toward the top of the vehicle and cutting from the windshield to separate the vehicle and dislodge the door.

That was something I could have never imagined before. Now, it's stuck in my memory forever. Those hydraulic rescue tools sent pulses through my body. The loud noises overwhelmed my senses. Shards of glass rained down on my face and my body from every direction. They covered me like pellets of ice, and they felt really strange on my arms and legs.

After the firefighters finished cutting the Jeep, they pulled me out and laid me on a board. First, they strapped my neck down with a neck brace. Then they taped me to the board.

Now that I was finally outside the Jeep, I had the first chance to look around me. I saw about twenty police cars, ambulances, and fire trucks.

Suddenly, a police officer appeared at my side. "What happened here tonight?" he asked, sounding rather concerned.

As I answered his questions the best I could, I figured out that the truck driver had fled the scene of the accident.

Not only did I have no idea where *he* was, I also had no idea where Gerard, Mike, and Tony were either. I didn't know if they were injured, or worse.

Because my head was stabilized to the board, I couldn't move to see what had happened to them. I was losing my mind trying to make sense of the situation.

Then, due to the extent of my injuries, the EMTs quickly shoved the gurney into the back of one of the ambulances. With a quick tap-tap on the glass, the rear EMT signaled the driver to *Go, Go, Go!* Sirens echoed around us as the ambulance raced the nine miles toward Jersey City Medical Center. I *knew* it was only nine miles, but it felt like it took nine hours. I tried to keep it together, but every bump, every pothole, felt like fire in my bones. I was nauseous. My head was pounding. My ears were ringing. My feet and my left arm felt like I had pins and needles. It was awful.

But as terrible as my situation was. I feared a worse fate had come for Gerard, Mike, and Tony.

Where are they? I was trying to figure it out.

The ambulance whipped into the emergency department unloading area and squealed to a short stop. The EMTs reversed their procedures in a rush, pulling the gurney and me out of the ambulance, onto the sidewalk, and into the emergency department.

The darkness outside compared to the bright lights of the hospital literally felt like night and day. My nervous system was already shocked and couldn't handle anymore, so I had to close my eyes. Even though I couldn't see, I was still aware of the medical activity all around me. The nurses and doctors moved fast—like a NASCAR pit crew, taking blood, placing an IV, inserting a catheter, all the while, bombarding me with questions.

"What happened?"

"Who was driving?"

"Can you hear me?"

"Can you feel your hands and feet?"

I tried to answer every question the best I could, but I was having difficulty thinking—and breathing. Although I was drifting in and out of consciousness, I could sense that panic was beginning to rise in the emergency department. I soon learned that my throat was closing because of the swelling in my spine. The nurses put me on assisted oxygen so I could continue breathing.

"Let's get an MRI, STAT!" I heard a doctor order. That's when I knew my situation was critical.

Even though they put a rush on it, it felt like I was waiting in that emergency room forever to get brought in for my MRI. At one point, I looked over and saw one of the officers I worked with at a nearby bed. He was escorting a prisoner admitted to the ER that same night.

"Aye, Goodie! You need help with anything while I'm here?" he asked.

I couldn't even grasp or articulate the specifics of what I needed in that moment.

A few minutes later, they administered a very strong pain medication in my system to relax my body, which was racing from the trauma it just went through. Staying awake was a battle I knew I was losing, so I gave in to the weight of my eyelids and fell into a restless sleep.

So much for stepping up to get us home safely.

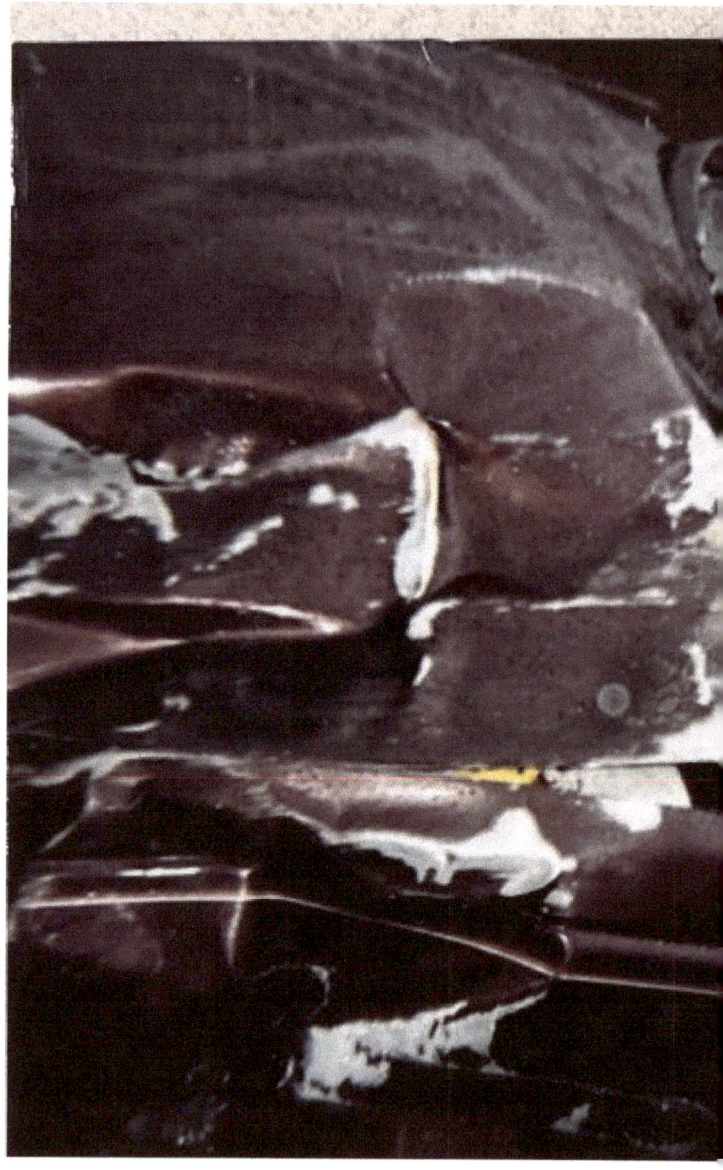

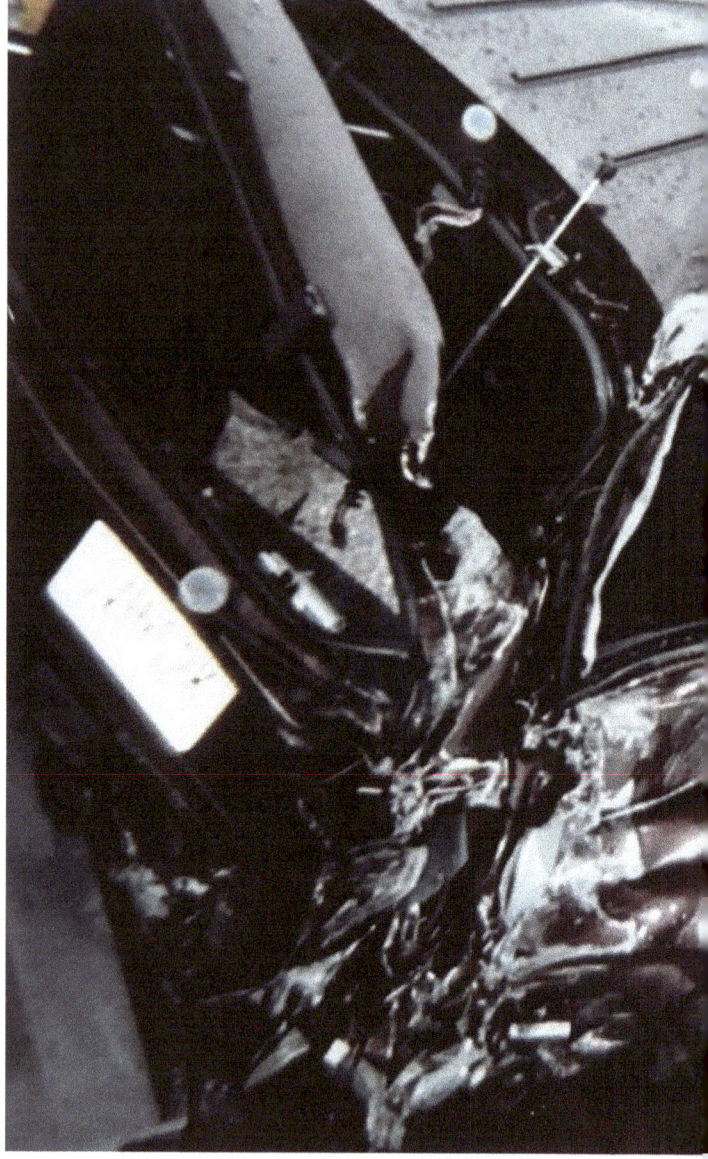

Chapter 2
The Diagnosis

The next few hours were a blur of white coats, muffled voices, and flashing monitors. Time crawled by painfully slow. Every second stretched longer than the last.

The emergency department felt like a war zone. I couldn't escape the bright lights, beeping machines, and shouting medical staff because I was still strapped to the gurney with my head and back immobilized. All I could do was stare straight up at the ceiling tiles like a prisoner of gravity.

I couldn't move my legs. My arms were starting to go numb. Even though I was hooked up to oxygen, I still had to gasp for breath. It felt like my body had forgotten how to breathe—the one thing it had always done without thinking twice.

"Why is it so hard to breathe?" I asked one of the doctors as I continued to struggle for air.

"The swelling from your neck injury is creating pressure on your spinal cord, which is restricting your breathing. Plus, your ribs are broken too," the doctor explained, a bit too relaxed for me.

Hearing the severity of my injuries was starting to hit me. I was feeling the pressure of every minute that passed, knowing that the stakes grew higher—and my chances of recovery fell lower.

But I still hadn't processed all of the doctor's words. Not yet. Not really. I think the shock was still providing a protective layer of hope—for some time.

Finally, after what felt like hours, a medical transporter wheeled me down for an MRI. My shoulders and chest were so broad that I barely fit in the machine. It was claustrophobic. At 6 feet tall and 248 pounds, I felt like a turkey in a microwave. The MRI techs kept pulling me in and out of the machine because the morphine caused me to get nauseous, and the tight space made it nearly impossible to breathe.

As my body strained against the walls of the machine, I was reminded of my physique. Strong. Fit. Honed from years of weight lifting and martial arts. I was desperately hoping that my training wouldn't fail me now.

But a little voice in my ear whispered, *All strength has its limits.*

Inside the MRI, the scanner hummed around me, taking snapshots of the damage that remained invisible to the naked eye. The seconds dripped by like a slow leak in the faucet. I felt tortured inside that chamber. Nobody knew the extent of my injuries, nor how long the road to recovery would be.

Finally, the buzzing finished. The test was over. When the medical transporter wheeled me back to the ER, I saw my coworker from earlier and asked, "Can you make a phone call for me?"

He nodded and said, "Of course."

I didn't ask him to call my family. I didn't ask him to call my job. I asked him to call Violeta—a friend I knew would show up for me and give me a ride home because I figured I'd be sent back with a couple broken limbs.

"Hello?" she answered on the first ring.

"Hey, Violeta. I work with Gary Good, and he was involved in a car accident. He's currently here at Jersey City Medical Center. I think he broke his arm and leg. He'll probably need some help getting home. Can you pick him up?"

"Oh my God. Is he okay?"

He replied, "I think so."

"I'll be over in a few minutes," Vi responded in her calm, usual manner.

I was then wheeled back into my all-too familiar emergency department bay. And I was alone again, staring at the ceiling.

I was spent. I closed my eyes again and drifted back to sleep. What could have been a few minutes to a few hours later, I heard soft footsteps enter the room. They were at a different pace from the frantic medical staff, so I glanced up and saw my friend Violeta gently walking in. We had known each other since I was seven and she was nine. I played baseball with her younger brother. We recently reconnected one day as I was walking out of my job. She had been visiting a relative at the correctional facility. We decided to keep in touch after that.

Vi was a sight for sore eyes. She was tiny—only 5 foot 1 with curly brown hair and soft brown eyes. She was now thirty to my twenty-eight years of age. I was so happy to see her. She was a great friend and one of those rare, special kinds of people in life who always come through.

"How *are* you?" Vi asked breathlessly as she stepped into the room.

"Not really sure," I said. "Just had an MRI. Can you find my brother, Tony, and Mike? I'm worried and don't know where they are."

Violeta checked a side room and found my brother awaiting medical attention, drifting in and out of consciousness. She learned that Mike and Tony had been treated for minor injuries but were not in the same emergency area. That gave me some relief. I tried to focus on breathing and waited for my MRI results. I wanted to speak to Vi, but before I could explain to her what happened, a doctor in a crisp white coat entered my emergency department bay.

"Are you Gary Good?" he asked.

I'm not even sure he heard me say, "Yes." Without introducing himself or even saying hello, the doctor announced, "You broke your neck. C5 and C6. You've sustained a spinal cord injury."

"Okay," I said, grappling to understand. "Can you fix it? When can I go home?"

The doctor didn't blink. He just stared at me, void of emotion. "You may not survive this injury," he said flatly. "And if you do … you'll never walk again."

The doctor's words hung in the air like a death sentence.

My body fell first. Then I felt my face drop. My head slumped over to one side. I tried to bring my arms and legs in toward my chest—an instinct to protect my heart. But my once strong, trained, and obedient body was failing me.

Then came the deeper fracture, the emotional one that doesn't show up on X-rays and MRIs: Doubt. Fear. Brokenness.

I started to cry.

A moment later, I heard familiar laughter. I glanced to my right, and there, two beds over, were Gerard and the boys. They were laughing and joking with each other.

"Hurry up! Let's get out of here," they said. They all walked away from the accident without a scratch.

I tried to shift my focus back to the doctor, who stood there in silence, avoiding eye contact with me.

I blinked back tears. "What does that mean?" I asked. "Like I broke my collarbone?"

The doctor slowly shook his head. "No. You shattered your vertebrae C5 and C6, which damaged your spinal cord. The trauma to your spinal cord is severe. There's compression and swelling. If we can't reduce it, it could be permanent." Then he repeated, "You may never walk again."

I stared straight ahead. I had no words. No tears. I felt a slow, painful unraveling of everything I thought I knew about my body. About my life. About my future.

It felt like I was listening to the doctor speak to me from the other end of a very long tunnel. Like the room wasn't real.

That's when I lost it.

The tears came suddenly and violently—like a dam bursting. I cried from pain, and I also cried from the weight of what had just been taken from me. In a split-second, I went from an officer who worked doubles, hit the gym, trained mixed martial arts, and raised his son on structure and hustle—to a man trapped inside his own body.

I couldn't even wrap my head around it. Somewhere beneath the tears, a different feeling began to take root.

Anger.

Not the kind you throw at people—but the kind you throw at God.

Why me?

That question screamed in my mind over and over and over.

I wasn't drinking.

I wasn't acting out or being reckless.

I was doing the right thing.

The loyal brother. The responsible man. The designated driver.

I thought of my son, Gary Jr, who was just eight years old at the time. Fortunately, he was with his mother that night, safe and sound in bed. I thought of our future together, just getting started, but now suddenly erased. I thought of us warming up before his baseball games, graduating to different belts in karate class, teaching him different lessons, making memories together. With. My. Son.

How was I supposed to show up now? What kind of example could I be in a wheelchair? It was too much to process.

I was blind-sided. I couldn't even begin to understand what my diagnosis entailed, let alone what my treatment and recovery might look like.

The doctor left without saying a word, giving me some time and space to gather myself. The room grew quieter, as both Vi and I were at a loss for words.

Moments later, another doctor breezed into my bay and announced, "Gary, you must have critical spinal fusion surgery to repair your injuries as soon as possible."

Then he continued, "But not yet! It's too risky. We need to stabilize you first."

The irony seemed to be lost on the guy. The doctors put me on anti-coagulants to reduce the chance of any blood clots forming.

They put me on pain medicine to reduce my soreness.

They put me on anti-inflammatories to take down the swelling.

Those medications were foreign to my body. Before my accident, I barely even took a Tylenol. The mixture caused me to stop breathing randomly in the middle of the day and night, which forced the nursing staff to rush in and help stabilize my vitals.

Breathing was challenging due to the fractures in my ribs; however, it appeared that they would be healing naturally, without intervention.

It felt like a bad dream.

Soon after, the doctors at Jersey City Medical Center told me that upon further evaluation, they determined that they couldn't do anything more for me there. I needed to be transported to the University of Medicine and Dentistry of New Jersey (UMDNJ) in Newark, New Jersey. They had a greater team of specialists, with experience in treating both spinal cord injuries and performing spinal cord surgeries. They were my best chance for recovery, considering the condition I was in.

I wasn't happy to hear about another transport, but I definitely understood we needed the A team on this.

Regardless of this change, they couldn't risk transporting me until the swelling reduced, my vitals stabilized, and my breathing returned to normal.

"That'll take about a week," my doctor said, without a tremendous amount of enthusiasm. I was sentenced to a week in that hospital. Silent.

Still.

Strapped to a board with a halo and a hard cervical brace.

And once again, staring at the ceiling tiles.

But at least I was upgraded from a bay in the ER to a hospital room in the ICU to await my trial.

On our way to the ICU through the hospital's maze of a hallway system, every stop and turn brought new sensations of pain. Because I was still unable to properly feel or move my arms and legs, a rotating cast of nurses and aides stormed in and out of my room. Like clockwork, they would "monitor" this and "adjust" that. Every hour brought a new medication, a new test, and new reasons for my growing uncertainty. The body that once obeyed my every command now betrayed me at every turn. I couldn't move by myself. I couldn't eat without assistance. I couldn't even get dressed or relieve myself unless there was help from the medical staff.

All I had left was the smallest bit of faith. And even that was getting harder to find by the minute. I grew up going to mass at a Catholic church with my family a few Sundays a month. I didn't have a personal relationship with God, but I knew He was there.

This isn't it. I can't give up. God won't abandon me like this.

I thought those words to myself with as much certainty as I could manage.

But my faith was starting to crack.

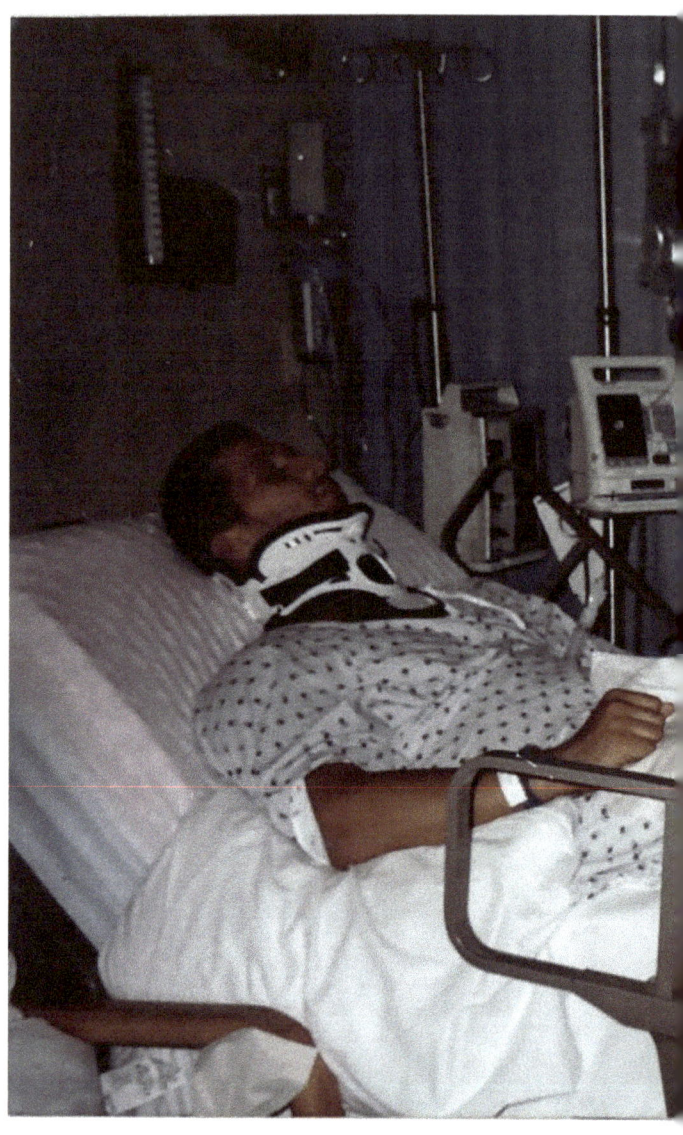

Trauma Center

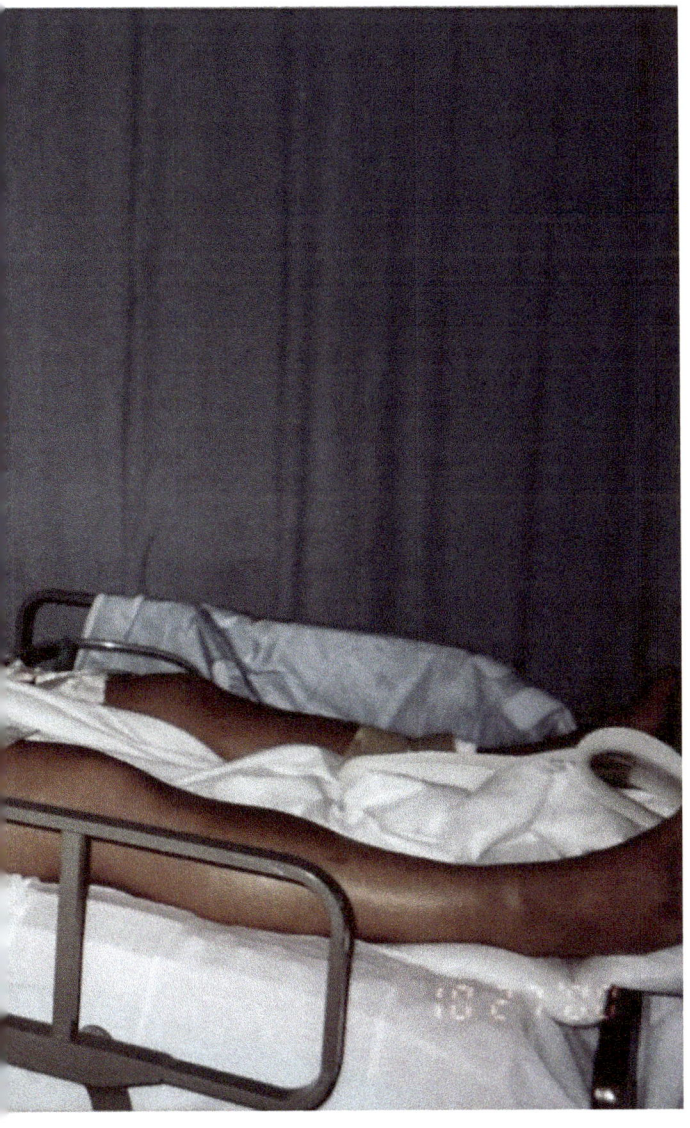

Chapter 3

Ceiling Tiles and Catheters

After my first night in ICU at Jersey City Medical Center, the reality of my situation smacked me like a freight train—first my mind, then my heart. I wasn't about to walk myself out of this prison of a hospital.

No matter how hard I tried, no matter how much my mind *yelled* for my body to respond, I was completely losing the ability to move from my neck down. Nothing felt or worked like it was supposed to. My arms were limp. My legs felt like they belonged to someone else. The connection between thought and action was cut off.

Plus, I had terrible pins and needles in my arms and legs, constantly. And there was nothing I could do about it. I couldn't use my hands. I couldn't lift my feet. I had to get comfortable with no longer having control over my own body.

But I couldn't accept the possibility that they might *never* wake up.

I laid still in that hospital bed, listening to the rhythm of machines: the swoosh of oxygen, the steady beep of monitors, the low buzz of fluorescent lights.

I stared up at the ceiling tiles, which became my unintended friends. The familiar, sterile squares reflected nothing back to me. Day after day, they were unchanged and unmoved by my pain. Like others in my position, I would sometimes imagine seeing tiny faces in the patterns on the tiles. My situation felt like it couldn't get any worse.

The minutes, hours, and days went by, blurring into one another. My hospital room was deathly quiet. But inside, my thoughts were deafening.

This can't be real, man.
Is it a dream?
Why can't I wake up?
This can't be my life.
Could the doctors be wrong?
They must be wrong.
They don't know me.
I'm different.
I'm a warrior.
I always get back up.

But anytime I managed to pump myself up with some positive thoughts, it'd be time to draw more blood. Followed by a catheter change. Then another concoction of medications that wreaked havoc on my digestive system. Doctors, nurses, and aides all briskly walked into my room—then they briskly walked right out. But I wasn't walking anywhere, never mind briskly walking. I was surrounded 24/7 by reminders that the life I once knew had been put on pause, and none of the staff believed I would ever be able to hit play again.

One thought played on repeat though—like that constant buzz of a fly in your ear.

You'll never walk again.

That sentence didn't just echo in my mind. It haunted it. With every IV drip, every nurse check, every body position adjustment, I heard it again.

My world was spinning out of control. This was a brand new—and uncomfortable—feeling for me. Self-control had *defined* my life. I grew up fast during a rough era. I was born at Bayonne Hospital in New Jersey on November 20, 1972. I was born to an Italian mother, Jean Good, and our Irish-English father, Charles Good, and raised with my brothers and sisters in the Marion Section of Jersey City. I learned how to hustle and defend the family before I learned how to write in cursive or do multiplication.

I got my first job in the second grade. By eight years old, I had a newspaper route in the Marion section of Jersey City for *both* the *Daily News* and the *Jersey Journal*. Plus, every other Saturday after my baseball practice during the summer, I helped my father clean cars at a used car lot on West Side Avenue.

My pops worked harder than anyone I knew and taught me that same ethic. He always let me hang around his friends so I could learn from the "old heads" and soak up game, instead of following the knuckleheads around my age.

By the time of the accident, at twenty-eight, I was a father, homeowner, correctional officer, and body builder. I was disciplined, focused, and built like a fighter.

Even though I was a young parent—just twenty when Gary Jr was born—I taught him the importance of speaking with respect, shaking hands, and making eye contact.

But now, nurses took turns rolling me around so I didn't develop bedsores.

Now, different aides had to change my clothes. Now, strangers had to help me relieve myself and clean up after me.

I'd never felt so exposed. So helpless. So vulnerable.

I used to hate asking for help. Now, I had no choice. Every time I had to humble myself and ask for assistance with basic human needs, I lost another piece of my dignity.

The nurses had inserted a catheter the night of my accident in the emergency department. The process was clinical, detached, emotionless, but for me, it was completely different. I felt humiliated. Every part of me that made me feel like a man had been stripped away.

Pride. Strength. Privacy.

Gone.

They taped me up, stabilized my neck, and ran more scans. Every nurse had a job to do. None of them made promises about my recovery. They barely even spoke to me.

During my week of purgatory at Jersey City Medical Center, I tried to call my son, but I had no idea what to say to him. What do you tell your eight year-old boy when your body won't move and your future's been rewritten?

So I waited.

And I watched.

Then I prayed—but not the kind of prayer I learned as a child in Catholic school. I didn't say the Our Fathers and Hail Marys I had memorized in the pews between my mother and father. This prayer was different.

It was the kind of prayer you whisper when no one's watching.

The kind that isn't prepared in advance, but formed in desperation.

It was a silent plea from a man hanging on by a thread.

God ... please.
If I can't walk, I don't want to live.
Please, let me walk again.
Please let me raise my son.
Just let me continue.

Chapter 4

The Unexpected Pain

As I laid in my bed at Jersey City Medical Center, I had plenty of time to think. By that point, I couldn't ignore the obvious. Two vertebrae in my neck. Not just *broken*. They were *shattered*. My spinal cord was being compressed like a garden hose that was run over by a dump truck.

A part of me was still in denial. Nothing but the pain felt real. Whenever I went to sleep, I prayed that I would wake up to my old life. I don't think my brain was able to accept the reality of what had actually happened to me.

One would assume that my injuries were agonizing. And they were. But it wasn't a sharp pain. It wasn't even a burn.

It was worse.

It was pins and needles, everywhere, all the time.

My entire body felt like it had fallen asleep but never woke up.

It felt like a thousand tiny needles were poking me from the inside out.

But, I couldn't scream because I didn't even have the strength.

The surgical team had to wait for the swelling to go down before they could operate. I learned that every hour they waited was a gamble because if the pressure didn't subside, it could cut off the nerves entirely.

Meanwhile, I was being heavily medicated. I was given blood thinners to prevent clots. Heavy morphine to dull the pain. And steady oxygen to keep my lungs moving. Every part of my body that once functioned without thought now required the full attention and management of a medical team.

I began to wonder:

Is this it?

Is this how I'll live for the rest of my life?

What kind of life is this?

Would giving up be better?

The physical pain was challenging, but the true struggle was mental—questioning my faith and grappling with anger toward God for allowing this kind of suffering. My uncertainty about the future caused a mental breakdown that was harder to endure than the physical pain itself. That was the unexpected part about facing destruction.

Seven unforgettable days passed as I waited to be told my body was strong enough for surgery.

Seven long days of silence.

Seven long days of machines breathing for me.

Seven long days of crying in the dark, pretending to be asleep when nurses came in.

On the eighth day, the doctors at Jersey City Medical Center ran another set of tests, which determined I was finally stable enough to survive the drive to UMDNJ. The hospital I was headed to in Newark, NJ, is a trauma center that specializes in spinal cord injuries. However, this next stop was part of a journey that I never signed up for.

Having grown up and lived in North Jersey my entire life, I knew that UMDNJ was a place for patients who needed more than recovery. It was for patients who needed a miracle.

The thirty minute ambulance ride to Newark was a nightmare. Every pothole felt like a sledgehammer pounding against my body. I vomited twice en route to the hospital. The EMTs kept asking me if I was okay, but truthfully, nothing was okay. And what could they do about it?

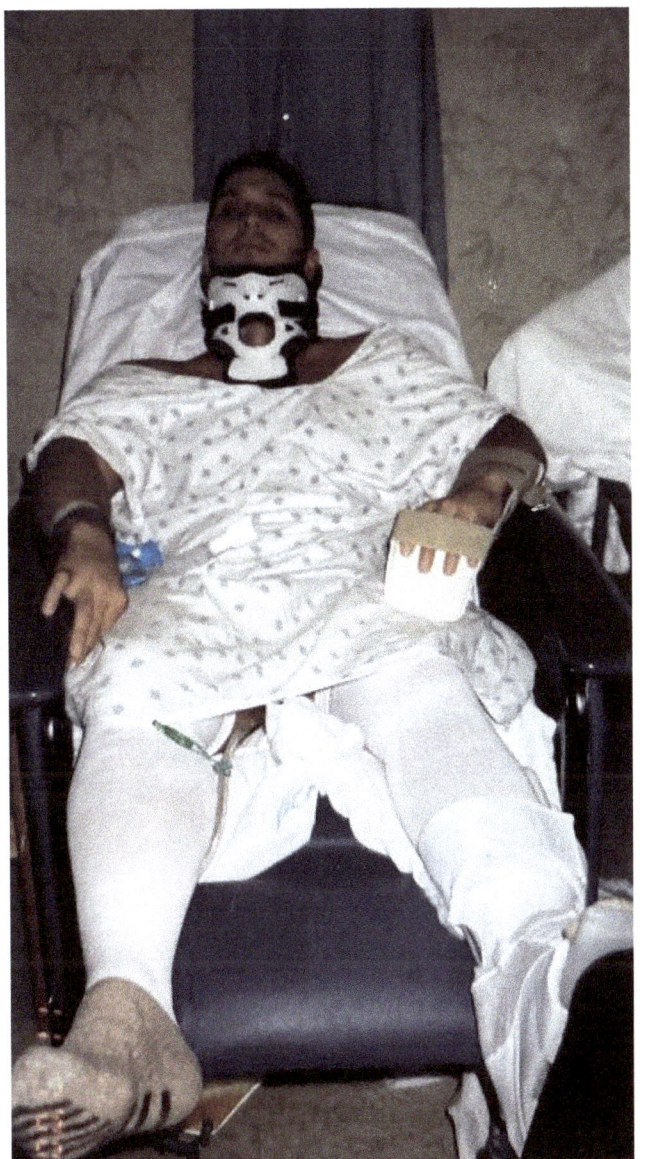

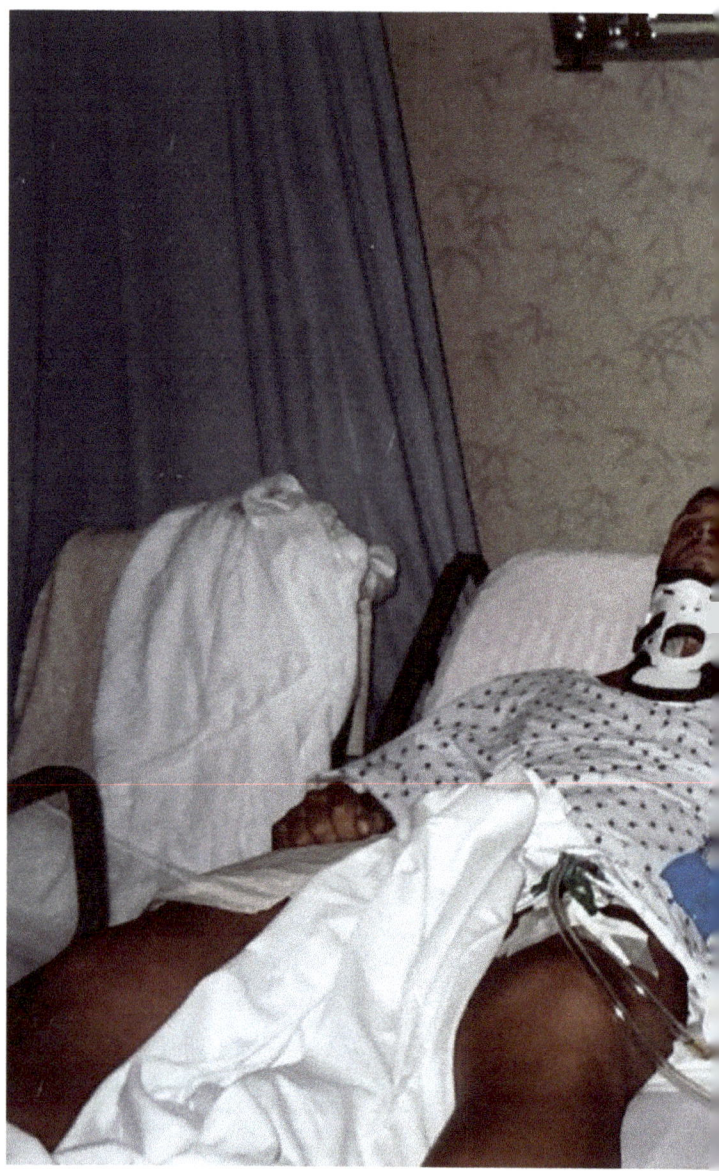

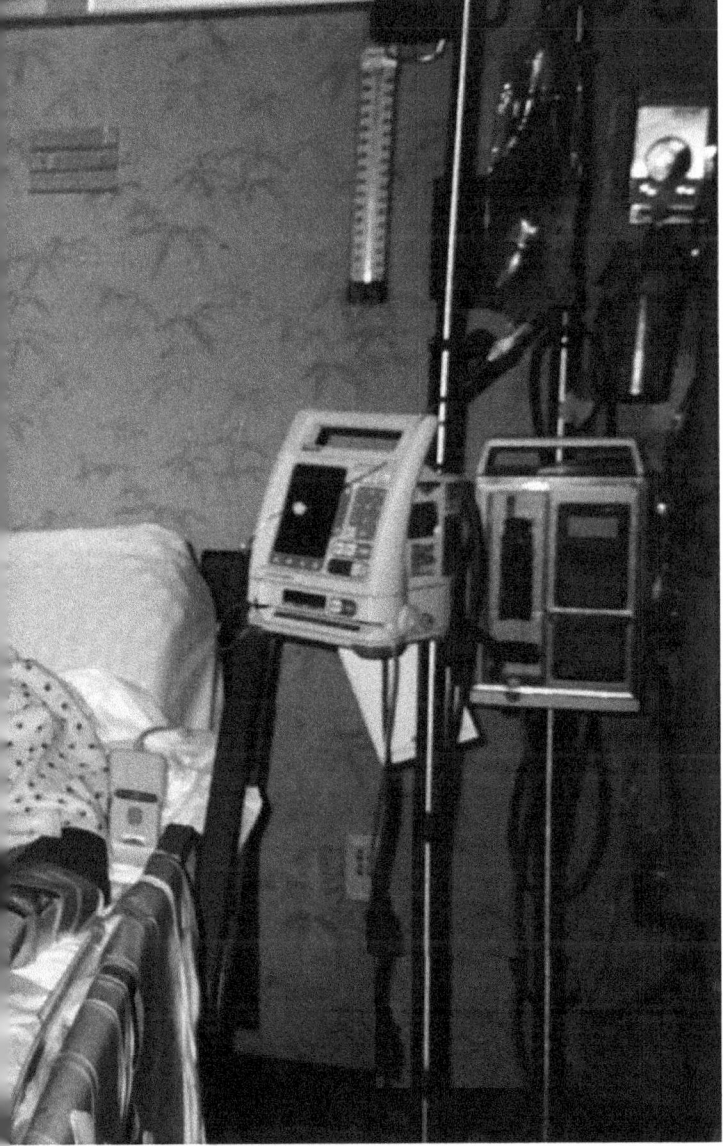

Chapter 5

Broken Bones and Borrowed Hope

When the ambulance doors swung open at UMDNJ and the EMTs rolled me out, I was no longer a man.

I was a case number.

A spinal cord patient.

Nothing more than a chart filled with red ink. Medical transport wheeled me through long sterile halls, passed patients in similar beds—bodies changed forever because of crashes, falls, violence, or just plain bad luck. It was a different kind of gathering: men and women whose lives had been rerouted by an accident, an illness, or fate.

No one spoke. But everyone was watching. The first stop was the ICU—where silence replaced conversation and monitors replaced familiar faces. My new room was dim. The walls were painted an off-white. I remember that color feeling colder than the air coming from the hospital's AC. I was still strapped to the board, neck in a brace, legs limp, catheter in place.

Thankfully, my breathing was improving now, but barely. My throat still fought for air every time I shifted—if I shifted, which was as little as possible because it cost me all of my strength. On top of that, it caused a tremendous amount of pain.

Machines echoed around me. Nurses moved in and out of my room like ghosts.

And then the doctor came in.

I caught the look in his steel-blue eyes. He had seen many men like me before. Dozens of them. And most of them never walked again.

He didn't say that up front. He didn't have to. I could feel it.

I was just another injury to him. Another body on a chart. Another spine he couldn't fix.

And he had probably spent years building a steel wall around his heart so he didn't have to feel the emotions that we all felt. The pain. The disappointment. The desperation. The hopelessness.

But what all of these doctors I would meet didn't know—what they couldn't see—was the war still raging inside of me.

I hadn't given up.

Not yet.

Not completely.

There was still something sustaining me that was stronger than the medicine.

Stronger than fear.

It was hope.

Faith.

Determination.

This isn't over.

This new doctor at UMDNJ repeated almost verbatim what the doctor at Jersey City Medical Center had said. But at least he introduced himself. "Hello. I'm Dr. Allen Maniker, the head neurosurgeon here at UMDNJ. I specialize in treating conditions like your spinal cord injury. You broke your neck, Mr. Good. C5 and C6 are severely damaged. There's swelling on your spinal cord. And right now, your body is paralyzed from the chest down."

He then paused, studying my blank stare. "You might regain some function. Or none. We don't know. We *won't* know until the swelling reduces. And we can't perform any type of surgery until then."

Some function. Or none. We don't know. What got me thinking about those words was how vague they were. Those words sparked some energy and a hunger for recovery. Those weren't medical terms. They weren't statistics supported by research and backed by science. Those were opinions.

I had built my life on discipline, structure, strength, and purpose. Now, whether or not I walked again, played catch with my son, drove my car, lived my life—*everything* depended on a vague maybe, from a total stranger.

I tried to nod.

But I couldn't.

***

I don't have many memories of my time in the ICU at UMDNJ. I struggled to remain conscious for most of my stay.

According to my medical records, I was placed under an induced coma so that my body would relax and have a better chance at recovering without involuntary muscle spasms. But I do remember the feeling of my father sitting next to me. My brain lit up with gratitude because I knew how much he hated hospitals—yet here he was. Right by his son.

As a result of this emergency, both of my parents had flown up from Fort Myers, Florida. My sister and her family, who were visiting my parents at the time, booked a flight as soon as they heard about my accident. That meant the world to me.

They said that Violeta had called my entire family and told them the news. The medical staff urged her to bring my next of kin because they didn't know if I would survive the next twenty-four hours.

I later learned that when Regina heard what happened, she couldn't contain herself. She jumped up and down, screaming, trying to figure out how to respond. She told me she remembers hanging up the phone and running to tell her kids, "We have to go! We have to go *right now*. Gary was in an accident!"

Her sons, Artie and Robert, were just young boys trying to enjoy a family vacation at my parents' home in Florida. They yelled back to their mom from the pool. "Aw, come on Ma! We just got here!"

Despite their plans for a vacation, everyone packed their bags, rushed to the nearest airport, and jumped on the next flight to Newark, New Jersey. It must have been exhausting for them having to travel with no clue of whether or not I would even survive the accident.

I could sense my parents standing at my bedside in disbelief. Regina was crying hysterically.

There were voices speaking, but they sounded so far away. I wanted to respond, but I was heavily sedated and felt like I was in an underground tunnel.

I heard my mom talking to me. "We're here for you. Everything will be fine."

My mother, who often went by Jeanie Mele, was my superhero. She raised seven of us: four boys and three girls. She was also a mother to the rest of the neighborhood, and her love extended to the entire community. She was always smiling, trying to help others, and raising us to prioritize the family structure.

My mom never complained about her problems. She wouldn't dwell on them either. She'd just continue moving forward like a machine, refusing to deny anyone assistance even if she needed some herself. She could do anything—painting, cooking, cleaning, helping neighbors, even caring for animals. No task was ever too difficult for her. She was an all-around great woman with the most compassionate heart.

"You're gonna beat this. I know you." I heard my dad say. "You got this."

My two motivators, my parents, on their wedding day

My father was a dedicated provider who worked two jobs religiously to support our family. We weren't well off, but he always made sure we had the essentials. His determination to provide demonstrated genuine leadership and set a positive example for us, his children. He was the type to show up for work even when he felt under the weather.

I remember briefly opening my eyes and seeing my parents looking down at their son, who was usually on top of the world but was now hanging on by a thread. I felt their fear in the air.

Later in my recovery, my parents shared with me that during their time in ICU, they reminisced on my athleticism, dedication to health and fitness, and warrior's spirit. They *expected* me to fight for my life. But as I reflect, I can't imagine how difficult it was for them to see me paralyzed, in a coma, and unable to speak with them as we always did.

***

During my stay at the hospital, as if the complete rerouting of my life wasn't enough of a surprise, the doctors discovered that I have an unusual blood clotting disorder. "An unintended diagnosis," they call it. I needed that about as much as I needed a hole in the head.

This blood clotting disorder is called Factor V Leiden. It dramatically increases my risk of blood clots. Immobile patients are susceptible to deep vein thrombosis—causing blood clots to form deep in the legs. So the doctors knew that in my condition, that risk was multiplied.

This caused another delay in my much-needed, critical surgery. Before the surgeons could stabilize my neck, they implanted a Greenfield filter to trap blood clots before they could travel to my heart, brain, or lungs and kill me. A Greenfield filter is a small, metal device shaped like a spiderweb. It was named after vascular surgeon Lazar Greenfield, MD, who collaborated with a petroleum engineer named Garman Kimmel to develop the filter, drawing inspiration from devices used in the oil industry to filter sludge.

Awesome. Just what I ordered.

The surgeons threaded the device through a vein in my thigh and up toward my heart. I prayed it did its job.

Although the insertion point in my groin was small, the pain was incredible. Every nudge of that metal web burned like fire under my skin.

Despite being paralyzed and unable to move, I could still *feel* everything in the area around the incision. The human body does what it wants. It can be alive in all the wrong places and numb where you need it most.

No medicine affected that kind of pain. Truth be told, the pain meds weren't working much at all. The doctors still had me on a shopping list of pharmaceuticals. Before the accident, my body was unfamiliar with drugs. But afterward, it became a medicine cabinet.

No matter what I tried, that pain just wouldn't disappear. I tried taking more medicine, but that just left me feeling out of it. As time progressed, I needed more and more meds just to get through the day. I started worrying about my body becoming addicted to the medication. I've seen friends struggle before, so I thought about how I could break away from this routine.

I laid there and dug deep. All of a sudden, I felt something convict me. That was God. He sent the Holy Spirit to help me fight through my circumstances. I was weak, but He met me where I was, at my lowest.

Although I tried not to complain, at night—when the lights dimmed and the footsteps faded—I would cry.

Not loudly. Not for attention.

But just enough to release the pressure building up inside of me. A man who'd never needed help before, now desperately seeking a hand.

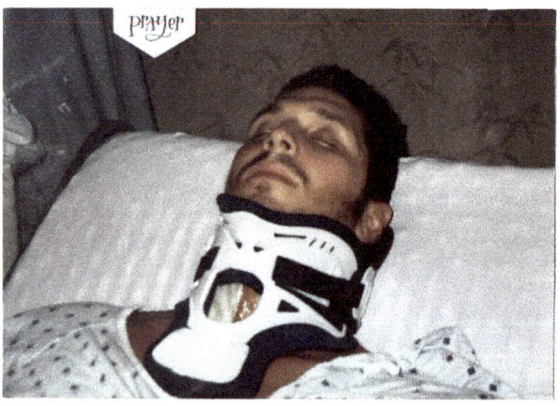

Chapter 6
The Loneliest Fight

As the calendar rotated through days, like hours, my family came and went. Doctors, nurses, and aides cycled through their shifts. My friends visited—frequently at first, but as it became clear my situation wasn't improving, they had to return to their day-to-day lives.

Only Violeta and Regina stayed and visited often.

Vi held my hand when I had night terrors. She wiped sweat from my forehead. She told me about her days and tried to lift my spirit with stories of life beyond the four boring walls of my hospital room. She listened to me on the rare times I had the inclination and energy to talk. And she sat in silence when there were no more words to say. Her presence was calm. Collected. Consistent.

But consistency couldn't make my brokenness disappear.

At night, the sadness, loneliness, and frustration ate at me until my brain fell numb and asleep. I would replay the accident over and over during my dreams. It was unbearable. Each flip of the Jeep caused me to jolt in bed, almost to the point of falling out of it.

Every day, I'd open my eyes to the same speckled ceiling tiles. The same broken body. The same buzzing from the machines and tingling in my legs that felt like fire and knives at the same time.

But what was even worse than that physical pain and discomfort was the pain of feeling I had been forgotten—by my body, doctors, loved ones, and even God.

All the training in the world couldn't have prepared me for that kind of loss.

The man who'd once worked 16's, trained at the dojo, and played catch with his son now had to be lifted like dead weight just to be washed and repositioned in bed.

And the shame. Sheesh, man.

That shame was a whole different pain. Needing assistance to use the bathroom was definitely the lowest point of my life.

Around the end of October 2000, fourteen days after the accident, the swelling was finally reduced enough to operate. My surgical team decided to schedule the spinal fusion.

It was an intensive surgery. Head neurosurgeon Allen Maniker, MD, reviewed the innumerable risks, including bleeding, nerve damage, and, of course, death.

What he left unsaid was the risk of *not* having the surgery: *You'll never walk again.* The doctor explained plainly, "Your injuries are so severe that we can't use the typical, synthetic hardware. The impact shattered your C5 and C6 vertebrae like glass. Instead, we need to harvest a strong, dense piece of bone from the crest of your pelvis to replace what has been lost in your neck."

Devastated, but grateful, my surgery was finally scheduled, and I *had* to be ready. After I was wheeled by a strangely cheerful transporter down to the operating room, a team of nurses lifted me onto the operating table. Then, the patiently waiting anesthesiologist put a mask over my face and gently said, "Count backward from ten."

"Ten … nine … eight ... zzzzzzzz"

They already briefed me on the surgery beforehand, so I had an idea what would happen next. The surgeons made an incision in my right hip. They shaved off a good bit of the durable bone. Then they strategically cut open the front of my neck, carefully navigated around arteries and nerves, and fused the hip bone to replace the shattered vertebral bones where my cervical spine was almost severed. To top it off, they secured it all back together with titanium screws and a cage to stabilize it in place.

Several hours later, when I woke up in the recovery room, I thought to myself, *What's going on?* I was still in denial, lost, not sure of what was actually happening to me.

I must have fallen back to sleep because the next thing I knew I woke back up in the ICU room. Dizzy. Swollen. Silent.

When I finally came to my senses, I was staring at something I could never imagine.

Eight women—friends, former flings, concerned companions—huddled around my bed. Some held flowers. Others held back tears. All of them waited to see what was left of the man they once knew.

This is unbelievable, bro. Did someone put them up to this? How did all eight of them know to come at the same time?

It felt a little bit like judgment day. At the time, I was single, and it was like every girl I was talking to was around the bed at the same time. My mom, my dad, and my sister, Regina, were there too.

All of the women were talking at once. Their loud voices were layered over one another's, so their concern started to feel overwhelming to me.

"What's going on?"

"What happened?"

"How are you feeling?"

"What do you need?"

While the women spilled over with words, I was limited with them. I replied, hoping to sound convincing, "I just need to rest. I'll get better soon."

I left so many things unsaid. I had no idea *how* I was going to get better. And although I wanted to get better in private, with my dignity like a man, that started looking less and less likely. Those realizations were very humbling for me. Never before was I unable to take care of myself.

Being vulnerable around my friends and family, especially the women, was the biggest blow to my ego. This couldn't be real. I was used to being "the man."

But in reality, as this struggle went on, the real man was always God. It took some time to understand that when I am at my weakest is when I can find His strength the most. He introduced me to humility. Looking back now, I know this was all happening *for* me, and not *to* me.

Truthfully, the more the journey unfolded, the more I realized that the strength I once depended on was never truly my own. It was always God's grace carrying me through the dangers of life. Each moment of daily struggle reminded me of my need for faith and who I needed to give all control to. I understand now that these challenges were quietly reshaping my spirit, teaching me to surrender and accept help from the one source greater than all others, Jesus Christ.

One by one, the women said their goodbyes and promised they'd see me soon, then left. By the end of the day, they all had left my side. Except one.

The beauty of that lesson wasn't about who *showed up*. It was about who *stayed*.

Violeta.

The one who wasn't asking for anything. The one who wasn't there for answers or drama or closure.

The one who simply stayed.

It was in that moment—as I wrestled with pain, vulnerability, and diagnoses—I noticed something changing.

Not just in my mind.

But in my heart.

I looked at Vi, who was sitting about a foot away from me on an uncomfortable pleather chair in my hospital room. The light coming in from the window caught her hair at an angle that created an angelic aura around her.

I knew Vi worked long hours as Chief Health Inspector of the City of Paterson, New Jersey. Yet *she* stayed. As a matter of fact, in the week that followed, Vi kept me company for hours every single day. She poured into me. She fed me home-cooked meals made by my sister, Regina, along with the massive goodie bags full of treats my sister sent. Regina made sure to include all my favorites. Dairy Queen slushies and sports drinks would also be packed and delivered weekly.

During my recovery after the accident, Regina stepped in like a second mother. She always went above and beyond, making sure I was cared for however she could. Her home-cooked meals brought me comfort when I needed it most, but it was more than just the food. It was her presence, her love, and her steady support that gave me that extra push I desperately needed. She never let me believe I was forgotten, and her selflessness during that time reminded me just how blessed I am to have her as my sister

My sister Regina and me

As I recovered, Vi was there to massage my legs and feet to help prevent any blood clots. She rubbed my scalp to calm my nerves whenever I needed it.

She stayed, for me, at my worst.

That made me feel valuable.

That kept me from going insane.

And that's when I fell in love with her.

***

The long-awaited surgery was over. It was successful.

But success didn't mean relief.

The pain had only just begun. Somehow, none of the team of doctors thought to prepare me for that. My body was literally hurting all over. The nerve damage I suffered was causing muscle spasms, twitching, and restlessness every time I fell asleep. My mind, body, and spirit desperately needed rest to recover, but this type of pain just wouldn't allow it.

My body was stitched back together—and screwed in place with titanium. Imagine that.

But my purpose?

My faith?

My will to live?

Those were still in pieces.

The doctors hadn't changed from their position that I would "never walk again." They hid behind their studies and statistics, which said fewer than one-third of people with incomplete spinal cord injuries will ever walk again. My injuries were so severe that my chances of walking again were even less than their data predicted.

But although no doctor would promise I'd ever walk again, there was something they couldn't research in a book.

I never asked *them* for a miracle.

I asked God.

And He wasn't finished with me.

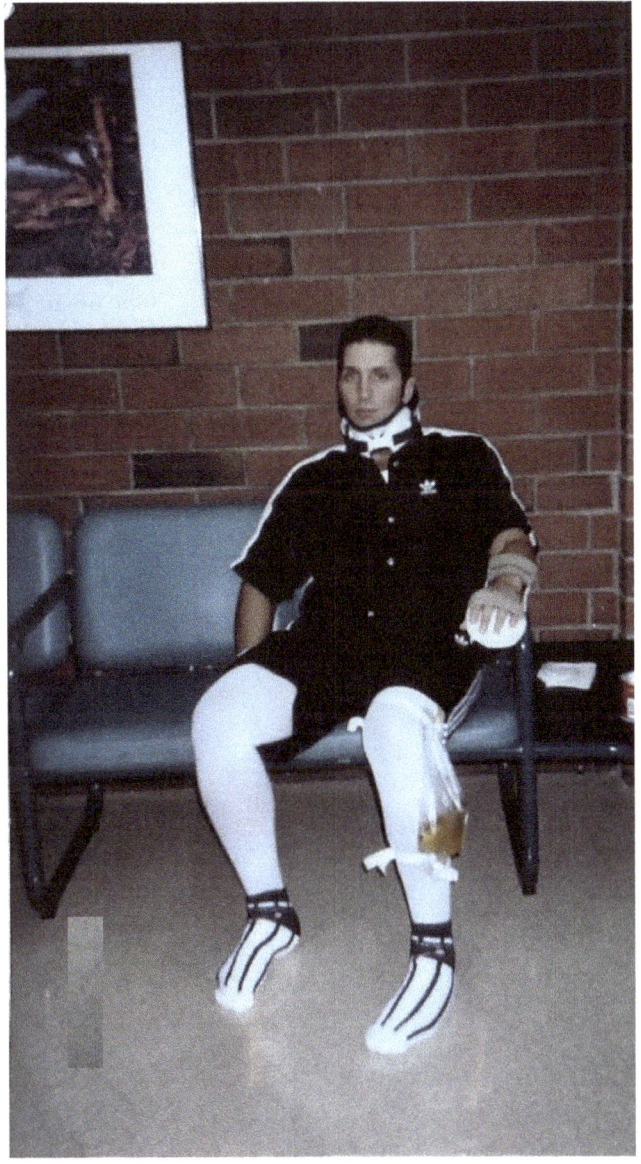

Chapter 7

The Room of the Unmovable

After working in the prison for many years and perhaps watching too many hospital dramas, I was well aware that once a patient had reached the end of the line and used up their last bit of hope with a hospital, they would move you to a different facility.

After two weeks of recovery in UMDNJ, the doctors confirmed that everything was in the correct place and the surgery was a success. They followed up with some additional testing before transferring me to Kessler Rehabilitation Center in West Orange, New Jersey. Later on in my stay, I learned that it's the same spinal cord facility that Christopher Reeves went to for therapy.

Prior to my accident, I had never spent more than a couple hours in a hospital. I had never ridden in an ambulance. By this time, I had been in three hospitals and three ambulances—and I didn't know how many more to expect. It felt like this nightmare would never end.

The ambulance ride from UMDNJ to Kessler wasn't long. But it felt like punishment. Even worse, banishment.

Every pothole, every time they hit the brakes, every vibration rattled the titanium screws that the surgeons just screwed into my neck. It was almost 2001, but the roads felt like we were stuck in the 1800s.

It was miserable. My stomach was in knots. The paramedics tried to calm me down, but I could hardly hear them over the pounding in my head and that voice reminding me: *You're not who you used to be.*

The paramedics rolled me through the front entrance of Kessler. It might have looked like a hospital, but it felt like a holding cell for hopelessness. The walls were gray and dreary. The floors were artificially shiny. The staff moved with quiet precision, as if volume might cause an episode amongst the patients.

Before the staff admitted me, they reassessed everything—yet again. More tests. More needles. More strangers looking at me like a file, not a father, or even a man. I wish I had felt like all of these tests were to benefit me. But I had the feeling they were due to liability.

Once I went through all the medical assessments for admission, they wheeled me into my room.

And it was not what I expected.

The room was massive. Wide open. And divided into four quadrants.

And in each of those four quadrants was a hospital bed. In three out of the four hospital beds laid three other men who, like me, had been told the same thing.

You'll never walk again.

No one had to tell me that the fourth quadrant was my new cell.

To my left was Eric, a young guy from the Jersey Shore. He was casually swimming when an undertow pulled him down. Just like that—his neck snapped, spinal cord severed, and he was paralyzed from the neck down. His breathing was shallow. He couldn't move his arms. His eyes barely blinked.

To my right was Reverend Conrad Jackson, a schoolteacher and part-time pastor from Newark. He'd been rear-ended by a stolen car on his way home from work one day. Another spinal cord injury. Another broken body. But Conrad brought something different into the room—scripture, peace, and faith. His Bible sat beside him at the ready like a shield.

And in the back, near the window, was John—a forklift operator from Saddlebrook, New Jersey, who'd fallen off his equipment, hit the ground hard, and crushed his vertebrae. He didn't talk much. He didn't have to. At nearly seven feet tall, he was a giant, now folded into a bed he could barely fit in.

The four of us were an interesting bunch of characters. The terrible irony of that sitcom was that the four inhabitants were prisoners in their beds. Only the people who *walked* in were able to *walk* out.

Silence was heavy in the room. It was only interrupted by machines and the occasional cough. There was no music. No laughter. Just stillness. And the question none of us dared to ask out loud: *Is this it?*

Kessler
°INSTITUTE FOR REHABILITATION
A Select Medical Hospital

75 years

Your path toward
recovery and
independence

Chapter 8

The First Three Months

My first few weeks at Kessler broke me down in ways that not even a high-impact crash with an 18-wheeler could manage.

Every day started the same: Nurses. Needles. Pills. Catheter checks. Injections of Lovenox into my stomach to prevent blood clots. Compression sleeves on my legs. Blood thinners. Ex-Lax. Colace. Repeat.

The staff called it *treatment*.

But to me, this was barely *surviving.*

My body wasn't just broken. It was literally dependent. Medications on top of medications to treat ailments and side effects, causing more ailments and more side effects. I was on the merry-go-round of medicine, and I couldn't get off.

At one point, one of the doctors at Kessler told me something that struck a nerve.

"It would have been better if you had been drinking."

"What do you mean?" I asked, feeling a little bit frustrated.

"In that vehicle, everyone who had been drinking was relaxed and passed out after the impact. Because you were sober, your instincts were to react and tense up, which made you most susceptible to injury."

That ignited a deep resentment down to my core. I wondered, *Why me?* I kept remembering how I had been at home sleeping, and my brother and his friends were partying and drinking. I was just trying to rest so I could see my son that weekend. *Why did I have to get hurt?* I was on an emotional rollercoaster.

God, I love you.
I always try to do my best.
I only wanted to keep them safe.
Why am I so broken?

It wasn't the pain that stung the most. It was hearing those words that broke my will to get up for a very long time.

Later on during my stay at Kessler, they performed a Doppler test and found a blood clot behind my right knee. They started injecting my stomach daily with even more Lovenox.

Every day began with injections and blood work. Needles shooting stuff in, and needles pulling stuff out. I had them for breakfast, lunch, and dinner.

You can't skip dessert though. All the medication I was put on, while being immobile on my back, caused my body to accumulate waste. In order to remove it, they fed me Colase and ExLax to target the buildup.

After I was at Kessler for about two weeks, I was finally able to use the bathroom. My younger brother, Gerard, helped me because I couldn't take care of myself.

Because everyone around me was so certain I would never walk again, they assigned me to therapy three times a week to condition me to living in a wheelchair. How could I hold on to hope that I might walk out of this place when every single patient in the entire facility was told by these doctors that they'll never recover their mobility? Being surrounded by all that negativity, especially during my first three months at Kessler, made me want to give up on living.

The curveballs didn't stop there. Despite all the medication I was being fed and injected with, I still developed a second blood clot. Except this time it was a DVT in my left leg.

I hadn't really moved in weeks. My legs were still numb. My stomach was bloated from medication. My back ached from lying in the same position.

The nights were the hardest. Sleep came in fragments. My only dreams were nightmares, and I'd often wake up mid-spasm, reliving the crash all over again.

Violeta stayed with me almost all day and night. She took a leave from work. She told me that when I would spasm in my sleep, it caused my body to bounce on the bed like a fish out of water. I couldn't stop replaying the impact in my dreams, the trauma, trying to fight when the Jeep flipped.

But there were positive signs. My arms were slowly beginning to return to normal. I could feel them a little bit, and they even started to move some. But even my arms twitched with painful muscle spasms that made sleep nearly impossible. Many times after an episode, I'd wake up to see my roommate Conrad in his wheelchair by my bedside in prayer. I listened to his prayers, but I hadn't experienced real conviction yet.

Truth be told, I didn't know how to pray. The first time I prayed with Conrad, I didn't even know where to begin.

"There's no right or wrong way to talk to Him," he assured me.

I began praying for God to give me the strength to overcome this so I could get up and continue being a strong leader for my family.

In a short amount of time, Conrad and I grew close. He often watched and spoke about Joel Osteen.

"I believe in Joel Osteen's words of encouragement, that 'God was good, all the time,'" Conrad said. "Dig deep during these times of trouble. We will overcome this!"

Conrad woke up a new hunger and desire in me to learn more about God's word and faithfulness. I even began tuning into Joel Osteen more. While I tried to bring a sense of humor into our stale, medicine-smelling, and depressing hospital room, Conrad infused the room with prayer, hope, and most importantly, God.

My time there was made bearable by my friendship with him. We were each other's eyes, helping one another navigate our shared room. After eating or having a snack, we would tell each other where the garbage can was located so we could properly throw things away. It was a simple act, but it helped us both get through the difficult times with a sense of humor and laughter.

One time, I asked the doctor for a prescription to get my legs massaged. Conrad immediately started teasing, convinced that was just my strategy to get free massages from the nurses. He'd mock me, saying, "There goes the white man trying to get a sister to give him a free massage!" He was certain I was faking the pain in my legs, and his humor filled my days with laughter. It sparked a friendly competition, and I kept an eye out for the opportunity to get him back.

One day, when my mom was bringing Conrad a rack of ribs, I made my move. While I was being wheeled out to physical therapy, I moved his garbage can without him noticing. Later, when he was enjoying the savory ribs, he wanted to throw away the bones and asked me, "Yo, Duke, is the garbage can close to this side of my bed?"

That was my chance. I told him, "Yup," even though his garbage can was nowhere near there. The ribs ended up all over the floor. When the nurses and aides walked in, they started yelling at Conrad and questioning him.

He immediately yelled back, "Gary told me the garbage can was near the bed!"

I was laughing so hard, trying to keep my composure. Through our friendship, and God, I felt a seed of hope being planted.

Those jokes weren't just about getting each other in trouble. They were our way of passing the time and focusing on something other than our diagnoses. The laughter we shared was truly the best medicine.

Not too long before my admittance to Kessler, my mother first introduced me to Joel Osteen. She was a true believer in God, and her faith helped me endure my condition with a smile. She had faithfully watched Joel Osteen's dad, Pastor John Osteen, until he passed to be with the Lord. From that point on, she never missed a TV broadcast with Joel, who took over as head pastor at Lakewood Church.

My mom's favorite words were, "God give me the strength." I kept that phrase in the back of my mind, even as a kid. I believed that must be true because God gave my mother the strength to raise seven kids and still find the time to serve others in the neighborhood.

So now, with Conrad constantly sharing how Joel Osteen delivered the gospel, that fire began burning even more for God's word. I started depending on God for the motivation to live, believing that only He can perform miracles.

I rejected every negative word the doctors and medical staff tried to declare over me.

Conrad and I started watching Joel on TV every week religiously. We prayed along with the program, hanging on to Osteen's words of encouragement, God's Love, and the message for the day. The quiet hospital room turned into our place of worship. We rallied together to overcome any and every obstacle that we dealt with mentally, physically, and spiritually. We gave all our burdens to God. Before that experience, I was used to relying on my own strength in the midst of a storm. I never knew we could go to God in our weakness to seek His strength and refuge.

Although I wasn't there yet, I was trying.

Trying not to give up.

Trying not to scream.

Trying not to believe the doctor who said recovery was impossible.

But more than anything, I was trying to survive my own internal dialogue that was struggling to remain positive.

Chapter 9
The Death of Hope

One morning, a few months into being at Kessler, a new doctor walked in. The tall, gray-haired physician bent down to look at some photos my family had taped to the side of my bed. It was a collage of pictures of me before the crash— healthy, strong, smiling, and standing proud.

The doctor raised himself to full height, peered at me over his wire-rimmed glasses, and asked in a stern voice that dropped the temperature of the room cold, "Who's that in the photo?"

"That's me," I answered.

"Hmm," the doctor scoffed. "Well, get used to the chair," he said, dismissively gesturing toward the photos. "You'll never walk again."

The doctor's words felt like being kicked while you were down. No empathy. No hope. Just a cold dose of "reality."

And it nearly broke me.

In that moment, everything in me died. That was the first time I actually wanted to give up. I stopped praying.

I stopped trying.

I stopped believing.

I just stared at the ceiling again—this time, not with confusion but surrender.

Little did I know … God Wasn't Done Yet.

The funny thing about God is that He doesn't always show His hand. He usually begins His work in silence.

And in that silence, something was taking place.

Not immediately. Not dramatically.

But slowly. And certainly.

Through Conrad and my family's quiet prayers.

And the return of strength in my fingers. Plus the faint voice in my head telling me, "You're not finished. I'm not done with you."

Despite everything in me falling apart and feeling defeated, a beautiful seed was being planted in a part of me that had been neglected for years. As a kid, I figured that church was about memorizing a book, putting on your Sunday best, and checking your emotions at the door like a coat. However, Conrad assured me that God has something different for us. Not religion, but relationship. I began learning how to pray from my heart. I couldn't get dressed up even if I wanted to. There was nowhere to hide. It was simply "come as you are." God never asked me to "check my emotions." Instead, He welcomed them.

Three months into my stay at Kessler, I bottomed out. I reached the lowest point of my journey.

Ironically, that's when the real recovery began—not just in my limbs, but in my spirit. Because without that, I had no chance at the road to recovery ahead.

Kessler
INSTITUTE FOR REHABILITATION

KESSLER
FOUNDATION

AND CAROLINE REYNOLDS
TER FOR SPINAL STIMULATION

Chapter 10

The One Who Saw Me

At Kessler, most of the staff followed the same rhythm. They were efficient, polite, and professional. They came in. Checked our vitals. Administered our meds. Reviewed our charts. Then they moved on. There wasn't much room for belief there. Just protocol.

But then came JR.

He didn't walk into the room like a therapist. He walked in like a teammate.

JR was broad-shouldered and athletic with the kind of presence that made you sit up straighter—even if you couldn't sit up at all. When he entered the room in February, he didn't start with paperwork or questions.

He looked at the photos still taped to the side of my bed.

I followed JR's eyes to see that one photo in particular caught his attention. It was one of me, standing tall in a crisp white tank top, holding a pair of boxing gloves. I had the body of a fighter and the stance of a man who'd taken hits and given them back.

"Was that really you?" JR asked, his voice revealing disbelief and respect.

"Yeah," I said quietly. "That was me."

JR nodded slowly, like he was envisioning a strategy.

"Well," he said. "Let's see if we can bring him back."

JR didn't wait for my permission. He wheeled me to the gym that day.

My roommates didn't come. Most patients stayed in bed. I didn't blame them. When your body stops working, your mind often follows. But JR refused to let me rot in that bed.

He started me slow—upper body exercises. Shoulder stretches. Assisted reps. Resistance bands. Pain. Sweat. Soreness.

It was like my muscles were waking up from a coma. They were angry, confused, and unsure if they were still a part of me.

But with every rep, something returned. And it wasn't just strength. It was dignity. After that, each morning, JR came to the room and wheeled me out personally. Not a nurse. Not an aide.

Him.

And that mattered to me.

I needed someone to see *me* and not just another statistic.

Therapy with JR became my new treatment plan, and I committed to it religiously.

Warm-up. Reps. Resistance.

Fall. Get up. Try again.

Fall. Get up. Try again.

JR was really into health and fitness, and he loved to work out. I shared my old work-out routines, my karate lessons, and more.

"Wow, man, you used to get it in!" JR said.

"Please get me out of this room, bro," I begged him.

JR continued taking me down to the gym every day he worked. He taught me some new exercises for my arms. But most importantly, he sparked that hunger for physical exercise again. I had given up on trying because I was in so much pain and frustrated that my body no longer worked like it used to. But JR reminded me of who I was: a warrior, built for the mountains *and* the valleys.

I usually exercised in my chair, but I eventually grew bold enough to tell JR, "I'm gonna try and stand up."

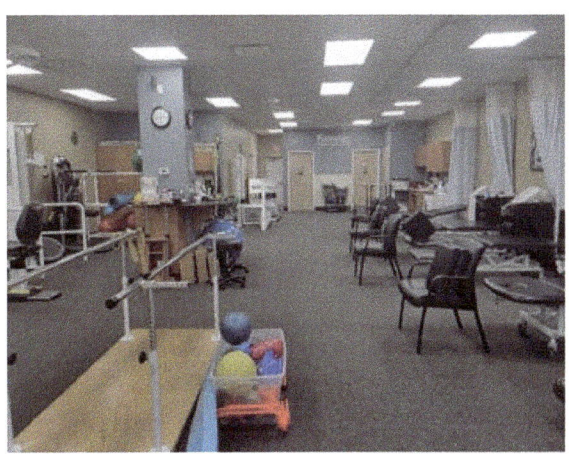

99

"C'mon, man! Let's get it," he replied.

Every time I was able to work my arms, I prayed to God to be able to work my legs too. JR began helping me to stretch them, and he encouraged me. That gave me hope.

The week after, when one of the doctors came to check on me, he said, "I saw you in physical therapy. How do you like it?"

"I love it!" I said.

"What are you doing down there?" he asked, looking a little too suspicious for my liking.

"I'm doing everything with my arms," I said. "Can you give me a prescription to exercise my legs and try to walk?" I knew that none of the patients at Kessler were allowed to do anything without a physician's prescription.

"I guess if you want, I could do that," the doctor said.

"I need you to do that," I responded.

And then, I got that prescription.

Clearly, God put JR in my life for a reason. Each day after our workouts when JR returned me to the room, my body ached, but my eyes were alive.

And the change wasn't just physical.

I even started praying more intentionally when I was all alone.

Not the memorized lines from my Catholic upbringing, but real prayers—raw, honest, broken.

God, grant me the strength to push forward.
Lord, protect my mind from disbelief.

I thank you for returning the feeling in my arms to me. And if it's in your will, please God, help me regain the use of my legs.
Lord, I'm not done fighting.
Use me.

***

By late winter, I was regaining control, movement, and strength in my arms. They were really coming back! I was finally able to hold a cup with my hand. Every day, I tried to pick myself up, and every day, I would fail.

I would fall face-first off the edge of my bed, trying to see if my legs had regained any feeling. The nurses would come in, strap me down, and ask, "Are you crazy? Don't do that!"

I knew I was rushing the process, but I had to take advantage of any effort my body was willing to produce.

A counselor was sent to meet with me and urged, "Please, be patient, Mr. Good. Don't try to rush our treatment plan."

I stared at her stoically.

I grew tired of being told to wait and be patient. The patient, patient? Patience is one thing, but waiting is not in my vocabulary. My only defense was prayer. Seeing a miracle like my arms regaining function was enough of a confirmation for me. I began to have a totally different outlook on my odds. Not everyone in Kessler was able to move their arms. This was a victory that God knew I needed desperately. A boost of morale.

If I could move my arms, what else could I do? Hope began swelling in my heart.

One afternoon in February, I asked JR, "Could I start practicing transfers—moving from the bed to the wheelchair without help?"

JR hesitated. "I'm not allowed unless I have a script from your doctor," he said.

I didn't argue.

I just started practicing after our workouts on my own.

Sliding toward the edge of the bed. Trying to plant my arms. Trying to lift.

Falling face-first.

Again. And again.

The nurses warned me. Yelled at me.

And threatened to strap me down.

I didn't care. I had to try. I had to fall. If I stopped falling, I'd stop learning.

Every day for weeks, when the second-shift nurses came on, they found me lying on the floor, face down, body trembling. They'd lift me back into my bed, shaking their heads.

But I wasn't embarrassed.

I was training.

***

And other patients in Kessler began to notice. I heard someone whispering, "That guy in Bed 2—the one they told to quit interfering with their treatment plan—was praying, lifting himself out of bed, falling on his face, then smiling and doing it all over again." None of it made sense, to anyone.

But hope rarely does.

Even JR started to experience a transformation.

He stopped using the word "if."

He started saying "when."

He began tailoring exercises for possibility, not maintenance.

By that time, I was proficient at sitting, and I was eager to try standing. JR continued to stretch my legs. Then he guided me toward a physical therapy device called walking bars, which I called a "guider." It consists of parallel bars and a mat underneath, and you gradually put your feet on it while holding yourself up. He shadowed every attempt I made to take a step and cheered me on to put one foot in front of the other. He said, "Come on, man, we are here to move forward, not to stay where you're at. Let's go!"

Those words hit my spirit and pushed me to force my legs to move, even if it was just an inch. For me, those were miles. For the first time in a very long time, I was standing upright on my own, and I knew the arm exercises were paying off. I was finally off my back and doing so while being "unassisted."

"Let's go! You gotta keep movin', G," JR urged.

I had been active my entire life, so those words were music to my ears.

From then on, we started trying new workouts. I told JR about how I would get out of bed and fall flat on my face.

"That's tough love," he said with a smile.

Being able to joke with him was good for my soul.

I was down in therapy every day faithfully. It started as only a one-hour session, then it became a two-hour session, and then three.

One machine allowed me to sit and let my feet hang down. I sat there for a moment. My feet hung beneath me, but they felt numb even though I was putting all my weight on the floor.

Then, all of a sudden, something new happened! I felt a spasm in my leg, but it was different from the usual ones. It wasn't violent and involuntary. It was controlled and felt more intentional.

We both celebrated and continued for a bit but then JR reminded me it was time to wrap up for the day. All I could think to myself was *"Thank you, God."*

Chapter 11
The Seed of a Miracle

A few nights later, after a long day of therapy, I slid my feet toward the edge of the bed again. The nurses were gone. JR had clocked out. The room was dim and quiet.

Although I was sore from all the training, I still had some energy to push my body further. The sensation I had been feeling in my legs was starting to change. I tried to mimic the exercises and bars from therapy to stabilize myself and feel the ground.

I pushed off with my arms.

And this time, when my foot hit the floor, it wasn't just numbness. The pins and needles felt a lot more dull compared to earlier in my recovery. I started checking both feet to make sure this was reality. Someone pinch me. I started feeling the pressure in my feet. The pain, the inflammation, the life…

This was it.

This was the moment.

The prayers with Conrad, the encouraging talks with JR, and the several falls on my face were actually coming full circle.

Gary Good

I wasn't walking yet. Not even standing. But for the first time since the crash, I wasn't just hoping.

I *knew* something was changing.

God was answering my prayers—not all at once, but steadily reminding me of his love along the way.

And for a man who'd been told he would never walk again, that love, revealed in miracle form, meant everything.

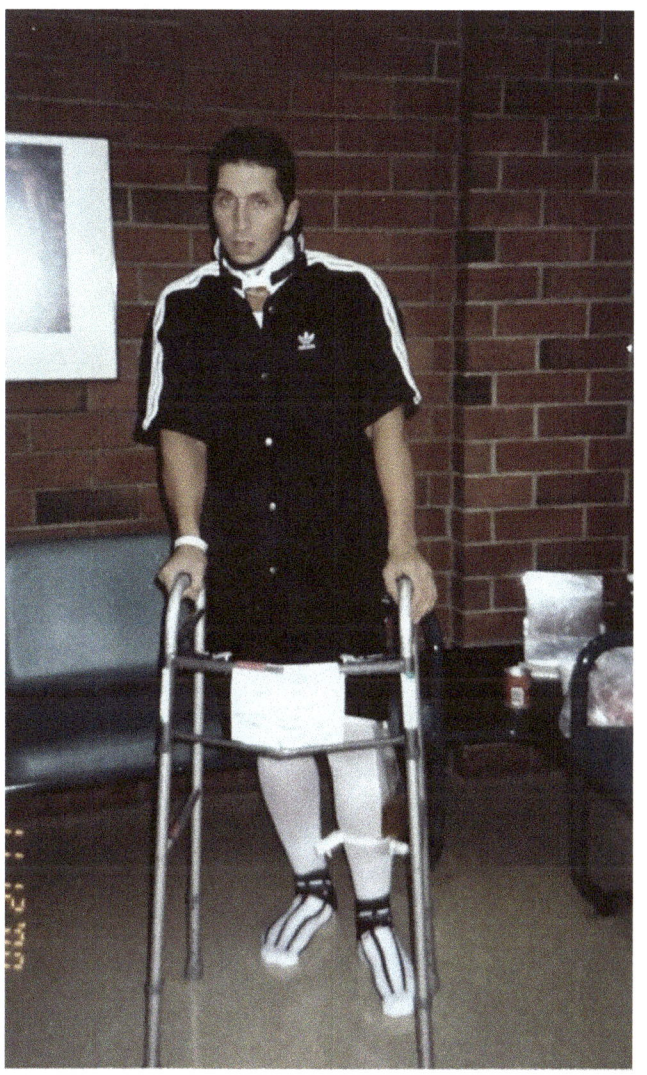

Chapter 12

Twenty Feet to Freedom

It started with pressure in my stomach. Not spiritual pressure. Not emotional.

Just that kind of pressure that required an immediate solution.

I had to *go*.

It wasn't the kind you can just ignore. It wasn't the kind you wait for a nurse to handle for you. This one was different.

It had been two weeks since I'd last gone. Every day, the nurses gave me laxatives, stool softeners, and some words of encouragement—but nothing moved. I was locked up from the meds, from the trauma, from the stillness.

But that morning, something shifted inside me. And not just in my gut.

My arms were stronger now. I could move myself in the bed, shift my weight, and prop myself up. JR's training was paying off. My daily falls were turning into calculated movements. I could feel something stirring in my legs—not strength, not control, but presence.

And today, I was done waiting.

The Slide

I didn't plan it.

There was no grand speech. No special thunder. Well, kind of. There was a pressure in my stomach, the kind that demands an answer. Two weeks of medication, muscle cramps, inflammation, and helplessness had built to this one moment.

Conrad was up early in his bed, reading scripture quietly to himself when he heard the sound.

I slid to the edge of the bed like I'd done several times before.

But this time was unique.

I maneuvered toward the edge of the bed, slow and steady. I was trying to remain focused even though I failed several times before, due to my unreliable body movement. I gripped the rail with one hand and used the other to push off from the mattress.

"Yo, Duke," Conrad said, using the nickname they'd started calling me. "Get down, bro. You're gonna fall again."

But I didn't pay him any mind.

I was locked in.

Feet dangling off the edge. Right one tapping the tile.

Left one twitching.

Then—another sensation.

I blinked, unsure of what had just happened.
Am I dreaming?
Am I hallucinating?
No.

I felt the floor against my foot.

My heart began racing, and blood rushed to my face like a heat wave.

And the bathroom—twenty feet away—called to me like the gates of heaven.

The First Step

One foot planted. Then the next.

Each sensation was a miracle wrapped in muscle memory.

I didn't think. I just moved.

It was awkward and all over the place. I looked like a baby giraffe learning to stand. But it was real.

Conrad watched from his bed, stunned. "Yo, Duke—Duke! Sit down, bro! You're gonna get us both in trouble!"

The Run

My legs began returning under me—not normally. Not fully under control. But present. Buzzing with electricity. Alive.

And this time, I wasn't falling.

I planted one foot, then the other. The cold tiles were refreshing to my soles.

I took a breath.

Then I sprinted—not athletically or gracefully, but epically. My legs moved, my arms pumped, and my hospital gown flapped behind me like a cape.

Conrad yelled from across the room. "Come on, Duke! You're gonna hurt yourself, man! Get back in bed!"

But I couldn't focus on anything but getting to that toilet.

My heart was pounding now—not from fear, but from fire.

I wasn't broken anymore.

I wasn't stuck in that wheelchair.

I was a miracle.

Something inside me had snapped loose. Or maybe it had finally snapped into place. It was only twenty feet, but to me, it might as well have been the Boston Marathon.

I was actually moving.

The world slowed around me.

The voices faded.

The beeping monitors silenced.

And there I was—

Running.

Not running from fear, but toward freedom.

Toward privacy.

Toward dignity.

Toward something I hadn't felt since the crash: Control.

I reached the bathroom, twisted the handle, opened the door, and sat down in relief.

No nurses.

No wheelchairs.

No help.

It was just me, my feet planted firmly on the tile, and a prayer answered in the form of twenty impossible feet.

I looked up.

Exhaled.

Cried.

Then laughed hysterically because I knew what God just did.

They told me I'd never walk again.

But that morning—alone, unassisted—I didn't just walk.

I ran.

They were wrong.

I wasn't another chart filled with red ink.

I was His miracle.

And everything was about to change.

With God, all things are possible.

Resources

These key resource websites helped and encouraged me daily during this journey.

Pastor Jon Schwartz and Pastor Alle Parker, Life Church-USA (Nazareth, PA and Macungie, PA)
www.youtube.com/@lifechurch-usa

Joel Osteen
www.joelosteen.com
www.youtube.com/@lakewoodchurch

Steven Furtick
www.elevationchurch.org
www.youtube.com/@elevationchurch

Joni Eareckson Tada
www.youtube.com/@JoniandFriendsVideo
joniandfriends.org
(818) 707-5664 | info@joniandfriends.org

Denzel Washington
www.youtube.com/@DenzelWashington
Motivationfans

Eric Thomas
www.youtube.com/@ApocMinistry
www.youtube.com/@etthehiphoppreacher
www.etinspires.com

Tony Robbins
www.youtube.com/@TonyRobbinsLive
www.tonyrobbins.com
Les Brown
www.youtube.com/@LesBrownSpeaks
lesbrown.com
Dr. Myles Munroe
www.youtube.com/@MunroeGlobal
Bishop TD Jakes
www.thepottershouse.org
http://www.youtube.com/@TPHDallas
Joyce Meyer
joycemeyer.org
www.youtube.com/@joycemeyer
Craig Groeschel
www.craiggroeschel.com
www.youtube.com/@craiggroeschel

My mother, Jean Good, and me in front of our family home on Wallis Avenue in Jersey City, New Jersey in July 2000

Special Thanks
to My Mother, Jean Good

My mother's name alone brings warmth to every chapter of my life.

She raised seven children, not with ease, but with an unshakeable grace that made it look easy. In a world filled with uncertainty, she was our constant—our lighthouse through every storm. Our home in every season.

There was no challenge too great, no task beneath her love. With scissors in one hand and a paintbrush in the other, my mother could transform a living room, a spirit, a life. She kept us fed, poured into us daily, filled our home with love, and still found the time to lend a hand to anybody in need. She didn't just raise a family; she nurtured a community. A mother not just by blood, but by heart.

My mother smiled in moments that would break most people. When life tried to wear her down, she stood taller. She was, and always will be, my superhero—made not of myth, but of flesh, faith, and fierce devotion. A woman with a heart of gold and the strength of a giant.

This book is for you, Mom. Thank you for being the reason I believe in love that endures, in sacrifice without complaint, and in the kind of quiet courage that changes the world one child at a time. May your spirit carry on through every page. I love you, Ma.

Special Thanks to My Son, Gary Jr.

Before the accident, being your father meant leading by example—showing up on the baseball field, at karate practices, and in every other physical part of your life. When I was paralyzed and the doctors told me I would never walk again, the deepest pain was not for myself, but for you. I was heartbroken by the thought that I wouldn't be the dad who could walk by your side, play catch with you, or guide you into the man you would become.

That hunger to be the father you deserved was my greatest motivation. It was a fire that burned brighter than any injury, and it pushed me to fight against the impossible. My faith told me God didn't save me just to leave me paralyzed, and you showed me the power of that belief.

You are not only the reason I fought to walk again, but you are also a co-author of this journey. You sat with me week after week, encouraging me to replay a painful past to create a story of healing and hope. This book is a testament to the life you gave back to me and to the lesson we learned together: **With God, all things are possible.**

I love you, and I dedicate this and every page of this book to you. Thank you for making my story and my testimony a book to share with the world.

Dad, "250"

Me and Gary Jr. in 2025

Special Thanks
to Joel Osteen

Joel Osteen's weekly encouragement to trust God's plan, to believe in miracles, and to never give up ignited a spark of faith that had been buried under confusion and pain. Through his ministry, I found the strength to overcome physical challenges, and I also discovered a renewed relationship with Jesus Christ. My heart, once heavy with grief and uncertainty, became filled with the hope and joy that only God's love can bring. It was words from my mother, Conrad, and Joel Osteen that planted a seed in me, which has continued to bear fruit in my life ever since.

Today, I am inspired to share my journey and testimony with others, on the miraculous ways God moved in my life before I was even a believer myself. From the accident that threatened to end everything to the vibrant faith that now defines my existence. I now put my trust in Jesus, "Our Lord, Our Rock." With a newfound purpose and a humbled state of mind, I pray that by sharing my story, I might offer encouragement and inspiration to other people who are facing their own battles, just as Joel Osteen did for me.

Special Thanks to Pastor Jon Schwartz, Life Church, Nazareth Campus, Pennsylvania

I would like to acknowledge and dedicate this page to our Lead Pastor, Jon Schwartz.

When I first started attending Life Church, I remember sitting in the service thinking, "Did my wife talk to Pastor Jon before this?" It felt like every word he spoke was aimed directly at me—so personal, so timely. But as I kept coming back, I realized it wasn't a coincidence. It was God, using Pastor Jon as a vessel to reach my heart. Through his messages, I was introduced to the Holy Spirit in a way I had never experienced before. I was moved so deeply that I gave my life to Christ.

Pastor Jon often says, "Love God. Love People. Do Something About It." That phrase stuck with me. It lit a fire in my soul to spend even more time with God and to share my story—not for my glory, but for His.

As I stepped deeper into *community* through groups like Married Life and Fight Club, Pastor Jon's leadership and authenticity helped me find healing and purpose. His teachings pointed me to God's promises and reminded me that restoration is always possible. Over time, I began serving and getting involved in church ministries—and I haven't looked back since.

I'm especially grateful for Pastor Jon's encouragement to "be the church" outside the walls of Sunday mornings. He often reminded us that our mess becomes our message, and that simple truth gave me the courage to write this book. His influence on my spiritual journey is undeniable, and I thank God for placing him in my life.

Pastor Jon, thank you—for leading with humility, for preaching with conviction, and for helping me see that God can use every part of our story. You've made a lasting impact on my life, and I'm forever grateful.

With love,
Gary Good
On behalf of the Good family

Special Thanks to Pastor Alle Parker, Life Church, Lehigh Valley, Pennsylvania

When my family relocated from New Jersey, we were stepping into a season of change filled with both excitement and uncertainty. More than anything, I wanted to find a church where my daughter would feel connected—where she could be part of a youth ministry that would surround her with faith, friendship, and a sense of belonging during an important time in her life. That desire led us to Life Church Macungie and, more importantly, to Pastor Alle Parker.

From the very first moment we met—during a Youth-United Night worship team practice—Pastor Alle stood out. His presence was genuine, his spirit was approachable, and his words were reassuring. He wasn't just "welcoming" in the casual sense—he made space for us, spoke to us like he knew what we were carrying, and somehow delivered exactly the kind of encouragement I didn't even know I needed.

Over time, he became more than just a familiar face at church. Through simple conversations and powerful moments, such as when he prayed over my daughter at her Sweet Sixteen, Pastor Alle poured into our family in ways that truly made a lasting difference. His leadership challenged me to step more fully into my faith and to live in a way that blesses others. He reminded me—with both words and example—of God's goodness, God's sacrifice, and the kind of love that builds community.

Pastor Alle, thank you for receiving us with wide arms and a sincere heart. Thank you for being intentional with your words and generous with your time. You've helped shape this season of our lives in ways I'll never forget. We are stronger as a family and closer to God because of how you've led and loved so well.

With deep gratitude,
Gary Good
On behalf of the Good family

Special Thanks
to Joni Eareckson Tada

This book is dedicated to an esteemed Christian who became a beacon of hope in one of the darkest seasons of my life: Joni Eareckson Tada. Several years ago, I experienced a life changing car accident—an event after which doctors told me I would never walk again. That season of pain, uncertainty, and limitation brought me to a crossroads where hope seemed unfamiliar. Yet, it was in that darkness that her story shone like light.

Through Joni's videos, writings, and testimony, I discovered a faith that refuses to be shaken. She showed me that even when the body is broken, the soul can rise with power, clarity, and mission. She spoke words of life, affirming God's truth in a time when despair tried to take hold. Through her unshakeable faith and unwavering joy, she reminded me that a life in a wheelchair is not a life without purpose—that God is our strength in weakness and our source of joy in every circumstance.

Joni's testimony pierced through my excuses and awakened in me a hunger for Christ like never before. I was struck not only by her endurance but also by her attitude of gratitude, her radiant joy, and her courage as an advocate for people with disabilities. After encountering her story, I began to see my own—a life redeemed for God's glory, where wounds became platforms for His grace.

Because of Joni's example, I found hope to continue the mission. I began to share my testimony, unfiltered and Christ-centered, and even to write this book. Despite what doctors once declared, I am walking today—not just physically but also spiritually, in step with the relentless love of Jesus.

Joni is a living example of courage, endurance, and faith. She didn't just pioneer a path for herself—she also held up a light for others, myself included, to find their way through very dark times.

I pray that my story too will encourage others as she encouraged me. I look forward to working with Joni and Friends in spreading hope and showing the world how God can turn our deepest wounds into testimonies for His glory.

With deepest gratitude and admiration, Gary Good

About the Author

Gary Good was born and raised in the Marion section of Jersey City, New Jersey. Growing up in a culturally diverse neighborhood with an Italian mother and an Irish-English father, Gary developed a deep appreciation for community, resilience, and hard work. The fifth of seven children, he distinguished himself early on as a talented athlete, excelling as a pitcher in both the West Side Little League and the Police Athletic League (PAL). He attended P.S. #23 and later graduated from Dickinson High School in Jersey City.

Driven by a lifelong passion for fitness and discipline, Gary pursued interests in weight lifting and mixed martial arts before transitioning into a career in public service. In 1994, he joined the Hudson County Correction Department, graduating from the academy and serving with dedication as a Corrections Officer.

A devoted husband and proud father of two, Gary's life took an unexpected turn when he suffered a life-altering injury that made doctors doubt he would ever walk again. His book chronicles this journey of perseverance and faith—an inspiring story of beating the odds, meeting God, and reclaiming one's self in the midst of destruction.

For daily devotionals, speaking engagements, and more, connect with me at: GaryGoodWWAP@gmail.com

YouTube
@GaryGoodWWAP
(Gary Good-Walking With A Purpose)

Instagram
@garygoodwwap

TikTok
@garygoodwwap

Facebook
@Walking With A Purpose

Coming Soon: Learning to Walk Again

After the miracle comes the real work. Now, Gary must prove he can stay on his feet—at home, at work, and in purpose. But his test of faith had only just begun.